Marriage 101

ALLISON & ALLEN

LOVE
DAD & MOM
26 JUNE 2012

Marriage 101

Building a Life Together by Faith

Jewell R. Powell

Revell

a division of Baker Publishing Group
Grand Rapids, Michigan

Published by Revell
a division of Baker Publishing Group
P.O. Box 6287, Grand Rapids, MI 49516-6287
www.revellbooks.com

Printed in the United States of America

Library of Congress Cataloging-in-Publication Data
Powell, Jewell R.
    Marriage 101 : building a life together by faith / Jewell R. Powell.
      p. cm.
    ISBN 978-0-8007-3332-2 (pbk.)
      1. Marriage—Religious aspects—Christianity. I. Title. II. Title: Marriage one hundred one.
BV835.P68 2008
248.8′44—dc22   2008041928

Contents

Acknowledgments

I would like to thank God for the gift of the Holy Spirit and the anointing through Jesus Christ that inspired me to write this book. Praise be to God!

I would like to thank my mighty man of valor, Lewis, for encouraging me to be all God has called me to be. Thanks to Lauren and Diamond, who probably don't even realize the sacrifices they made so that I could accomplish this project. I love you, and I thank God for blessing me with you three wonderful gifts.

I also would like to thank the following people:

- My parents, Della and Johnnie Jones. I thank God for you and what you have done and taught me over the years. I love you both very much.
- My mom, Ann Wheeler. I love you and I thank you for your love and support.
- My sisters and brothers: Tuffie, Carla, Al, Lowell, April, Michael, Antionnette, Shanea, Elvin, and Shonté, whom I love dearly.
- My husband's sisters and brothers: Mike, Jeff and Susie, Robin and Arnold, and Lee. Thank you so very much for believing in me and supporting me.

- Robin Dessau—thanks for being a cousin, proofreader, and best friend.
- My loved ones, who have stuck by me through thick and thin: Kim Best, Danielle Finney, Patrice Pullen, Kim Shepherd, Crystal Simmons, Lawanne Stewart, and Leslie Taylor.
- Pastors Ervin and Shona Fields for their permission to use information from their VCMI Marriage and Ministry Manual.
- My editors and all those who prayed for me—thank you.

Preface

A long time ago, I met my Prince Charming at a Roy Rogers fast-food restaurant. After dating for three years, we decided to get married. We were both aware of the statistics concerning marriage, and we both had parents, siblings, and friends who were divorced. We were very concerned and cautious about marriage because all around us were divorced couples. We had a little over three months of premarital counseling and a couple of months to prepare for the big day. Because we did the counseling, attended church regularly, and felt a strong love for one another, we believed we were ready for marriage and would be fine.

So Lewis and I pledged our love until death before a host of family and friends on May 4, 1996. Immediately we started having problems, one of which was infertility. Then, a couple of years after our wedding, Lewis stopped going to church while I remained a faithful, active member. Within four years we found ourselves sleeping in separate bedrooms, not liking one another very much, and estranged as a couple. I quickly found out that marriage was nothing like the fairy tales I read as a child. Lewis and I thought we had done everything necessary prior to getting married. We thought we were well prepared before entering into marriage.

In February 2001, I was in a dark place in my life. Lewis and I had just separated, and all I knew was that I loved my husband but our marriage was not working. I started wondering why so many marriages, including mine, were heading toward divorce. Is it possible to live in holy matrimony until death? My Christian faith had me searching for answers. Because I believed in God's Word, I knew I would find the answers in the Bible. What I learned was that with man (you or your spouse), it is impossible to have a happy, satisfying, and fulfilling marriage, but with God nothing shall be impossible. The Bible says, "For with God nothing is ever impossible and no word from God shall be without power or impossible of fulfillment" (Luke 1:37 AMP). We can find hope in knowing that the same God who is the creator of marriage and the one who unites couples can help us keep our marriages strong and bless them.

If you are going through hard times in your marriage right now, there is hope. There is nothing wrong with the institution of marriage; actually, it's very good if you do it God's way. The problem is with us, because we don't understand why God created marriage or even how it works. God created the covenant of marriage. So we need to let go of preconceived ideas we've learned from the world—from television, movies, books—and the ideas and goals we had when we were growing up. Whenever we make a purchase (be it a computer, stove, car, toaster, or camera), we get instructions—a manual—and a customer service number to help us understand how to use it. Yet when it comes to marriage, God's institution, we go not to his Word but to magazines, books, and psychic hotlines. But the Bible is our manual.

Most of us have heard what the acronym BIBLE stands for: Basic Instructions Before Leaving Earth. The Bible gives us everything we need to make it in life, especially in our marriages. God says his people perish because of the lack of knowledge (see Prov. 29:18). Marriages are destroyed because people lack knowledge of what God says in his Word concerning them. Why would God create marriage if it couldn't possibly work? He wouldn't, and he didn't. It's not the marriage covenant that is the problem; it's those who don't seek God and get their wisdom, knowledge, and understanding from his Word.

My prayer for everyone who reads this book is that the Word of God will come alive to you and cause you to want to change. The purpose of this book is to lay a spiritual foundation. As you read it, God will give you (by the leading of the Holy Spirit) answers concerning your marriage, just as he did for me. If you will change your thinking and incorporate the truth that God will show you, your marriage *will* turn around, just as mine did. My marriage started improving after only two months because I did everything God told me to do. You have to purpose in your heart to submit to the Lord and to do all that he tells you to do concerning your marriage. Is my marriage perfect today? No, but it is so much better, and with each passing day it gets even better.

The Purpose of This Book

Marriage 101 was written for anyone who wants their marriage to be strong and healthy and is seeking a better relationship with their spouse. This book is a combination of book and workbook that is designed to help you examine areas in your life that need to be changed in order for you to have a successful and fulfilling marriage. By doing the exercises, you will begin to see God's plan for your marriage. They will help you to develop godly character and build your marriage upon a strong foundation. Ultimately, if you truly yield yourself to the change process, you will be transformed into Christ's image because you will be focusing on the vertical relationship between you and God rather than the horizontal relationship between you and your spouse.

At this time you may be going through a "wilderness experience," which I define as having problems in your marriage (such as adultery, not getting along, one of you wanting to leave, or having feelings of loneliness or depression). Perhaps you're about to give up because it seems as though there is no hope.

I've heard many stories from failed marriages. Here are some of the reasons and excuses I've heard for getting married and then not staying in that marriage:

I'm not getting any younger.
I'll try it out and if it doesn't work, I'll leave.
I'm lonely.
He (or she) will change once we get married.
I'm pregnant.
I married the wrong person.

I could go on, but there is no point, because this book is for those who want a better relationship *regardless* of why they got married. In my own life, my marriage was almost destroyed because I sought to come up with my own solutions rather than seeking God concerning the problems and challenges we were facing. He is the one who designed, purposed, and ordained marriage from the beginning. Marriages are ending at an alarming rate, both inside and outside the church, because we don't understand that *change* is mandatory when bringing two completely different individuals together to become one in God.

Even if your marriage was built upon the wrong foundation (without Christ), this book will help you to fix that crumbling foundation and make it strong. If you are contemplating marriage, this book will prevent you from building your marriage upon any foundation other than Jesus Christ and the Word of God. And if you already have a good marriage (or even a great marriage), it will help you to develop a closer relationship with God and your spouse. (Note: If you are in an abusive situation, I suggest finding a Christian counselor to give you the support you need and help you seek God as to what you should do concerning your situation.)

God never intended for marriages to end in divorce. In Matthew 19:3–8, the Pharisees asked Jesus whether it was lawful for a man to divorce his wife for any reason.

> Jesus replied, "Have you not read that he who created them from the beginning made them male and female? For this reason a man shall leave his father and mother and be joined to his wife, and the two shall become one flesh. So they are no longer two, but one flesh. What therefore God has joined together, let no man separate."
>
> Then the Pharisees asked, "Why, then, did Moses command to give her a certificate of divorce and send her away?"
>
> Jesus replied, "Because of the hardness of your hearts Moses permitted you to divorce your wives, but from the beginning it has not been this way."

Divorce was never the intention of God. Our heavenly Father has given us every piece of marriage advice and counsel that we will ever need to have successful marriages. It is all in his Word. Therefore, no matter what is going on in your relationship right now, know that you alone cannot turn your relationship around, but "with God all things are possible" (Matt. 19:26).

When my marriage was in ruins, I knew deep down inside that my husband and I had purpose as a couple. I knew that divorce was not the right thing to do or the answer to the problems we were facing. God had something great for us to do! I had no idea at that time, when I was ready to give up and in desperate need of help and answers, that God would use us to help other couples in similar situations.

But God had to change me before I could begin doing the things he was calling me to do. Before you begin the journey of your own transformation (change process), know that it will *not* be easy. It will take work, commitment, and Jesus on the inside of you in order for you to see the fruit of your labor. I challenge anyone who truly wants to be used by God and to fulfill his purpose in your life to do all the things God is telling you to do concerning your marriage. If you do, the blessings from your obedience will be phenomenal.

If you truly want to be changed (conformed to Christ's image and likeness) and you want your marriage to be heavenly, you must be willing to do the following:

Be honest with yourself.

Stop looking at your spouse—what they are or are not doing.

Do all God is telling you to do (even when your mind is screaming "no!").

Constantly pray and seek God for answers.

Take your time. Don't rush—change is a process!

Change, change, change—stop making excuses.

Are you willing?

How to Use This Book

This book provides an eight-part plan that you can study on your own or in a group. Take your time in working through it. Tailor your study time to fit your life and situation. Don't put a timeframe on how long it should take to complete each chapter. Please understand that this book is really about examining the areas in your life that you need to change. "All scripture is given by inspiration of God, and is profitable for doctrine, for reproof, for correction, for instruction in righteousness: That the man [and woman] of God may be perfect, thoroughly furnished unto all good works" (2 Tim. 3:16–17).

I wanted this book to include practical tools to help you reflect upon the wonderful lessons you will learn while God is speaking to you through each chapter. Each chapter will set forth a goal in terms of developing new attitudes and behaviors based on biblical standards. These goals are summed up in the acronym ALTRUISM:

Act
Love
Talk
Repent
Unite
Identify
Submit
Minister

The word *altruism* means an unselfish regard for the welfare of others. It sums up who Christ is and why he died for us. Therefore, I used this word as an acronym to help you develop godly behavior according to God's Word. The acronym ALTRUISM, broken down and used throughout this book, describes how one should Act, Love, Talk (or communicate), Repent, Unite, Identify, Submit, and Minister in a biblical way to your spouse and loved ones according to the Word of God. The goal is to always think about what you do and how that affects your loved ones and then develop the godly behavior to help you improve those relationships.

Each chapter concludes with a "Why should I" question to challenge you to think about why you should act in the biblical manner being discussed. Throughout my own transformation, I kept asking God why: Why should I love my husband the way God was teaching me to love him, especially when I felt that my husband didn't deserve it? Why should I submit to a man who was not even serving God? I questioned everything. These sections will help you understand why we should develop each particular behavior. God wants all of us to have a victorious life and win souls for him.

Each chapter is followed by a workbook section that will help you to understand more clearly what is being discussed in that particular chapter. The workbook sections will help prepare you to be what God wants all of us as Christians to be: a light in a dark world. Each workbook section includes several parts designed to help you learn more of what Scripture says about that chapter's subject and apply it to your own life and marriage. Below are the elements that are included in each chapter's workbook.

Biblical Example

These sections profile good and bad examples of married couples in the Bible. Although I provide a summary of each story, I've also referenced where you can find the entire story in the Bible. Read the full story and allow it to further help you improve your relationship with God and your spouse.

Scripture Meditation

"This book of the law shall not depart from your mouth, but you shall meditate on it day and night, so that you may be careful to do according to all that is written in it; for then you will make your way prosperous, and then you will have success" (Josh. 1:8 NASB). Since every part of *Marriage 101* is supported by Scripture, I urge you to meditate on all of the Scriptures provided to you. It is important that you don't overlook them so that you may hear what God wants to speak directly to you through them. I encourage you to read and reread the Scriptures listed in each Scripture Meditation section, underline them in your Bible, and meditate on them so you can get a greater understanding of what God is saying about your situation. Space is provided under each Scripture reference for you to write in your own words what God is saying to you.

Self-Examination

The questions posed in this section allow you to examine yourself. They are designed to help you reflect upon the mistakes made in your marriage and to highlight the areas that you need to change. Notice I said *you*, not your spouse. You must be willing to stop playing the blame game and to take an "up close and personal" look at yourself and what you must do in order to see your marriage turn around.

Developing Character

This section is designed to help you develop godly character. Each one provides an assignment for you to work on in order to help improve your relationship with your spouse and others. Make the commitment to develop godly character in your life, which is the necessary ingredient for turning a failing marriage into a great one. Matthew 7:24 says that the one who *hears and does* what Jesus says is like a wise man who builds his house upon a rock. That is the goal: to build or rebuild our relationships upon a rock—a strong foundation in Christ.

Of course, you cannot work toward this goal in your own strength. That is why each chapter includes a prayer. This prayer is an opportunity for you to come into agreement with God concerning changes necessary in order for you to see improvements in your marriage. Make a decision that you will hear and respond to what the Holy Spirit tells you throughout this transforming process.

Affirmation

The affirmations are Scriptures rewritten to help you speak by faith. As you say them, you may not feel that these things are true about your marriage; however, saying them will help you to change your thinking and see your marriage in a different way.

Reflections

This section is designed to act as a journal. It is a place for you to write down and reflect upon all the things that God spoke to you while you read the chapter and worked through the workbook. Take advantage of this area to write down God-inspired notes that you will be able to reread for years to come.

My Prayer for You

As you prepare to begin *Marriage 101*, here is my prayer for you:

Father, I lift up every person who is seeking your will for their marriage, and I come into agreement with them right now that their lives and marriages will be forever changed. I agree with them that they will have godly marriages, the way you designed them to be—marriages made in heaven, here on earth, right now! Because I see the greatness of your plan by which they are built together in Christ, I bow my knees unto the Father of our Lord Jesus Christ, of whom the whole family in heaven and earth is named, and ask that you would grant, according to the riches of your glory, for them to be strengthened with power by your Spirit in their inner man, so that Christ may dwell in their hearts by faith and they may be rooted and grounded in love and experience a type of love that they cannot fully comprehend—the breadth and length and height and depth of God's love in them and working through them (as your Word says in Ephesians 3:14–19). In Jesus's name, amen.

Introduction

A Sleeping Beauty Parable

As I was writing *Marriage 101*, I was led to revisit the story of Sleeping Beauty. After reading the story and then watching the movie, the Lord showed me that this fairy tale is a parable of Christ's love for the church. Jesus taught in many parables throughout his ministry, and even today we are able to receive revelation from them.

What is a parable? A parable is an earthly story with a heavenly meaning. The story of Sleeping Beauty has a valuable hidden meaning that can be revealed to you if you allow the Holy Spirit to show you. Then you will see the timeless story of God's eternal love for mankind and the sacrifice his Son, Jesus Christ, made over two thousand years ago by willingly dying on the cross to save mankind from their sins.

Before we begin our journey, allow me to set the stage for you and share the revelation the Lord gave to me about this classic fairy tale. Although the story is about a princess who falls in love with a prince, the underlying story is how the prince sacrificed his life for her and what that sacrifice accomplished. For those who might not be familiar with the Sleeping Beauty story, here it is in a nutshell.

The Story of Sleeping Beauty

Once upon a time, a king and queen celebrated the long-awaited birth of their daughter. It was a joyful day, and feasts were thrown throughout all the land to pay honor to her. All the people in the city brought gifts. Another king presented his son, and both monarchs prayed that their kingdoms would one day unite through the marriage of their children. In honor of the baby princess, three good fairies descended from the sky to give three special gifts. The first gave the gift of beauty. The second gave the gift of song. But before the third could give her gift, an evil fairy appeared in a blaze of fire.

The evil fairy was upset that no one had invited her to the special celebration, and in her anger she cursed the baby, saying that before she turned sixteen, she would die by pricking her finger on a spinning wheel.

Needless to say, the king and queen were quite upset. To comfort them, the good fairies reminded them that the third fairy had not yet given her gift.

The king and queen exclaimed, "Can you reverse the curse?"

"No," the good fairy replied, "but I can modify it. Instead of dying, she will sleep until true love kisses. Then she will awake."

No one—neither the king nor the good fairies—could reverse the curse. Only true love could revoke it. In an effort to save his daughter from pricking her finger, the king made a decree that all the spinning wheels in the city should be burned. The townspeople brought their spinning wheels and threw them into a bonfire.

In the meantime, the good fairies tried to find a way to harm the evil fairy. However, they realized they could only do good; they had no evil in them. So how could they stop the evil one from hurting her? One of the good fairies came up with an idea. The one thing they knew about the evil fairy was that she didn't have what they had—love. The evil one didn't know or understand love or any of the characteristics that make up love.

In a vain attempt to protect their daughter, the king and queen decided to keep the child hidden and safe until she passed her sixteenth birthday. As part of their plan, the good fairies would live like mortals to raise the princess in a hidden place. While in hiding, the princess had to live as a peasant girl, which was beneath her birthright.

For many sad and lonely years for the king and queen and their townspeople, their beautiful princess remained hidden. During those hidden years, the princess continued to grow and mature into a beautiful young woman. Although she appeared on the outside as if she had everything, she was lonely. She was not living in the fullness of who she was as a princess, and she had not yet met her true prince.

Then the princess met a man, whom she did not know was a prince, and they fell in love. The prince rushed to tell his father how he had fallen in love with this peasant girl. But his father, the king, was very upset with the news. A peasant girl?

The princess also ran home to tell the good news that she had fallen in love. To her surprise, she was told of her identity—that she was a princess, not a peasant—and was taken to meet her family. Before she could see her parents, the evil fairy put her into a trance, and she followed a spirit until she came to a spinning wheel.

A voice said, "Go, touch it," and the princess pricked her finger—just as the evil fairy had said she would—and fell into a deep sleep.

The good fairies didn't know how to tell the princess's father the terrible news. Instead, they put the whole kingdom to sleep. One act—a finger pricked on a spinning wheel—put the whole kingdom to sleep. However, before the king fell asleep, the prince's father tried to tell the other king that their kingdoms would not unite because the prince had fallen in love with a peasant girl. One of the good fairies overheard it, and immediately she knew that the prince was the princess's true love.

To thicken the plot, when the fairies arrived at the cottage where the prince was, they found that the evil fairy had already taken him. Now they would have to go to the forbidden mountain to help the prince. At that time the evil fairy and her ugly creatures were celebrating with fire and laughter. They were teasing the prince, who was in the dungeon in chains, about true love *not* conquering all. When the good fairies reached the prince, they told him that they couldn't help him because the powers of the evil one were great, but they could give him a shield of virtue and a sword of truth, which they called the weapons of righteousness, to help him triumph over evil.

After receiving these weapons from the good fairies, the prince proceeded to do exactly what they had told him to do. When the ugly creatures came against him, he fought them off one by one. As each shot their fiery darts, the darts hit his shield and turned into flowers. The evil creatures pushed huge boulders off the top of the mountain to crush the prince, but before the rocks could hit him, they turned into bubbles. Then, as the prince galloped on his horse toward the gate, they dropped hot molten lava at the gateway. But a rainbow suddenly appeared over the exit, and the lava didn't touch him.

The prince finally made it out from the dungeon and away from the evil one, but the evil fairy put up a barrier—a forest of thorns around the castle—so he couldn't reach Sleeping Beauty, who was lying asleep inside. The prince began cutting and chopping his way through the thick forest of thorns.

All of a sudden the evil fairy turned into a dragon and told the prince that he would now have to deal with all the powers of hell. The fight was intense, and the dragon seemed to be winning the battle. Although the prince was obviously exhausted and appeared to be overcome by his enemy, he continued to persevere. He fell down and got back up and fell down and got back up. He even lost his shield. Then the fairies cast a blessing on the sword so that evil would die and good would endure. He threw the sword at the dragon, and it struck the dragon in the heart.

Recognizing the Symbolism

Now let's look at the story again to see its biblical symbolism. Sleeping Beauty (the princess) represents the church—she is the bride. The prince represents the bridegroom—Jesus. The princess is "sleeping" as a result of the curse that is put upon her, which represents darkness and is symbolic of man's sin, rebellion, and ignorance. In John 12:35 Jesus says that he who walks about in the dark does not know where he is going. He is drifting. The evil fairy represents Satan, and her ugly creatures represent demons. As we know, light represents truth, goodness, and the kingdom of God.

Just like Sleeping Beauty, mankind was under a curse—sad and lonely for years—because of the sin committed by Adam and Eve. We were in darkness and no longer had a direct relationship with God. Why? Because Adam and Eve's sin was disobedience, and sin separates us from God. When a person has not yet met or developed a relationship with the Prince of Peace, although their lives may appear on the outside to have everything, they are not living in the fullness of who God has called them to be.

The fact that Sleeping Beauty is raised as a peasant girl is also symbolic. Every time I read that Sleeping Beauty was a peasant girl, God reminded me of the gift of salvation that was given to the Gentile nation through the redemptive blood of Jesus Christ. Although the Jews were God's chosen people under the old covenant, anyone who accepts his dear Son, Jesus Christ, has been adopted into his royal family under the new covenant. God instructs us in his Word, "But ye are a chosen generation, a royal priesthood, an holy nation, a peculiar people; that ye should shew forth the praises of him who hath called you out of darkness into his marvelous light: Which in time past were not a people, but are now the people of God: which had not obtained mercy, but now have obtained mercy" (1 Peter 2:9–10). The two kingdoms in the story represent two nations, the Jews and the Gentiles, which are now united as one because of the noble actions of the Prince of Peace, Jesus Christ. Under the new covenant, there is neither Jew nor Gentile but one body under the leadership of the Lord Jesus Christ (see Gal. 3:28). The three fairies represent the Holy Trinity (Father, Son, and Holy Spirit).

In this story, the beautiful princess is put under an evil spell. God showed me that just like the evil fairy put the curse on Sleeping Beauty, Satan put a curse on mankind. When the serpent deceived Eve and she and Adam ate from the forbidden tree (see Genesis 3), sin entered into the world. But the third good fairy brought comfort, saying that while the curse could not be reversed, it could be changed. I see this as the Holy Spirit giving comfort, just as Jesus said he would do: "And I will pray the Father, and he shall give you another Comforter, that he may abide with you for ever" (John 14:16). The Greek word for "comforter" is *parakletos*, which literally means "one called alongside to help or an advocate." The Holy Spirit is called "another" comforter because, as 1 John 2:1 states, Jesus himself is our advocate.

The third fairy's solution used the power of love, which the evil fairy did not have. My Bible defines the fruit of the Spirit as "love," which is made up of the following characteristics, as stated in Galatians 5:22–23: *Love* is the willing, sacrificial giving of oneself for the benefit of another without thought of return. *Joy* is gladness of heart. *Peace* is tranquility of mind, freeing oneself from worry or fear. *Long-suffering* is patience with others, a disposition quietly bearing injury, the opposite of a short temper. *Gentleness* is kindness. *Goodness* is generosity. *Faith*, in this context, means dependability, faithfulness. *Meekness* is humility—being teachable and thinking of others before your own needs. *Temperance* is self-control or the ability to control your desires. In our own lives, these are the characteristics we need to beat Satan at his deceitful tactics. As born-again believers, we must overcome evil with good!

The very nature of God is love. If we respond to the evil one with God's love, then Satan is paralyzed and unable to retaliate, because we have just stopped him in his tracks. This is how we can keep the devil out of our marriages, out of our homes, and out of our lives—by walking in God's character. Love is a powerful weapon.

Love is also seen in action through the fairies who hid the princess away to protect her. Jesus, too, gave up his birthright and lived as a human here on the earth to accomplish God's perfect plan to save mankind from their sins.

The love between the prince and the princess is symbolic of God's powerful love for us. I am reminded of what Scripture says in 1 John 4:19: "We love him, because he first loved us." When the prince met the princess, he was so excited that he didn't care about who she was or where she came from. Our Prince, Jesus, feels the same way about us when we receive his love and accept him as Lord and Savior of our lives. He doesn't care who we are, what we've done in the past, or what sins we are committing. He just loves us and receives us as we are. That is what is so awesome about the good news of Jesus Christ.

Sleeping Beauty isn't just a fairy tale. As I was watching the movie, the image of Sleeping Beauty being lured into a curse by an evil spirit was an awakening moment for me. I realized that the voice of the evil fairy was the same evil voice that told Eve to eat from the tree of the knowledge of good and evil. It is also the same voice that tells you and me to do something that is contrary to what God is telling us to do.

The prince trapped in the dungeon—a symbol of hell—is a picture of Jesus descending into the lower parts of the earth (or hell; see Eph. 4:9) to strip the enemy of everything he had stolen from God so that it could be restored to us.

When I saw the fight between the prince and the dragon, the Holy Spirit gave me a vivid picture of what our Prince, Jesus Christ, had to endure before ascending to the right hand of the Father. We have to realize that it was only Jesus—not the angels, not the Holy Spirit—who had to go to hell, defeat the devil, and save his beloved (you and me) from her sin. I could see Jesus literally fighting Satan in the kingdom of darkness, destroying all the works of the devil, triumphing over sin and death, reclaiming everything that rightfully belonged to God, and reconciling mankind back to the Father. All that Jesus endured and the benefits of the price he paid on the cross are available to anyone who accepts him as Lord and Savior of their lives. That is why the gates of hell cannot prevail against us—because Jesus has already won the battle. Thank you, Jesus!

Just as the fairy-tale prince was given weapons of warfare against evil, so God gives *us* weapons of warfare. Ephesians 6:10–17 confirms that the spiritual weapons given to the believer will help us triumph over evil. The *helmet of salvation* protects the mind from Satan's lies. We put on the *breastplate of righteousness* by reminding ourselves that God looks at us through Christ's righteousness; therefore, we are not condemned when we do something wrong. We can repent and move on in our righteousness. Just as Jesus allows us to go free without guilt and shame from our sins, in the marriage covenant we must learn to implement the same practice with our spouses. We put on the *belt of truth* by learning what the Bible says so that when the enemy attacks, we'll know the truth of God's Word and it will hold us up. The *sword of the Spirit* is the word (or guidance) God directly gives you pertaining to a particular situation. For example, if the enemy is attacking you in your marriage, and God has already given you a word about that situation, you fight the enemy with that word. Then strap on the *shoes of the gospel of peace*, knowing that you can stand firm in the battle against Satan. Hold the *shield of faith* high by putting your trust in God for victory when Satan attacks and tries to defeat you. This means that you won't doubt what God says, because you take him at his word and believe his promises. Scripture says, "Above all, taking the shield of faith, wherewith ye shall be able to quench all the fiery darts of the wicked" (Eph. 6:16).

Just as the prince used his weapons to slay the evil fairy, as believers, we must slay evil with the spiritual sword given to us. We must use the Word of God to cut down the cares of this world with which Satan tries to entrap us.

We Have the Victory

Just like the prince in this story, you may be in the midst of the worst battle of your life right now, and you may seem to be losing that fight. Just know that the Word is blessed. According to Mark 11:22–24, if you have faith in God and don't doubt in your heart, you can have what you desire. You have already won! The victory is yours if you just hold on to God's Word and what he has spoken to you. We can have confidence because our Prince of Peace has already defeated the enemy. Because of his actions, we are destined to overcome and win, no matter what situation we may find ourselves in. We *will* triumph over the enemy.

In the Bible, Jesus promises that the gates of hell shall not prevail against the church (see Matt. 16:18), which gives me a picture of the church going on the offensive and the devil being on the defensive. Since the devil has no authority over us, we can aggressively attack and snatch what belongs to us, including our loved ones, out of darkness into God's glorious kingdom of light.

In the tale of Sleeping Beauty, immediately upon the death of the dragon, the kingdom was no longer in darkness. The weeds and entanglements of the forest were gone, and the sun came out in all its brilliance and glory. The prince had beaten the evil one. The curse was now reversed. This scene demonstrates what happens when you first receive Christ as your Savior. Before you come to Jesus, your life is in total darkness and your heart is entangled in a forest of sin. Then you hear the message of the gospel, and God's love immediately comes into your heart. The darkness that once clouded your life is now overpowered by the radiance and brilliance of God's glory—his presence. You are immediately removed from the kingdom of darkness, and the enemy of your soul is defeated. You are now a born-again child of God. Thank you, Jesus!

The prince ran to his beloved and sealed his love for her with a kiss, and she was awakened with love in her heart. Instantly all the people throughout the city were awakened too. The prince and princess were married, the two kingdoms were finally united as one, and they lived happily ever after. Unlike this fable, however, Jesus's fight against Satan was only the beginning. He hadn't finished God's work. In order to unite the kingdoms—in order to allow all people to enter the kingdom of heaven—he had to seal the new covenant with his blood. Ephesians 2:11–22 describes this uniting, and verse 16 says, "And [He designed] to reconcile to God both [Jew and Gentile, united] in a single body by means of His cross, thereby killing the mutual enmity and bringing the feud to an end" (AMP).

Why did Jesus die? One, that all people throughout the earth (Jews and Gentiles) could partake of God's love through the gift of salvation; and two, to end the feud for our souls once and for all.

Ephesians 4:10 (AMP) says that Jesus died that he might fill all things (from the lowest to the highest). What are just a few of those things? He died so that:

- sin would no longer dominate us, because we have forgiveness;
- Satan would be defeated, and we would rule and reign over him;
- we would no longer be subject to death, because we have eternal life;
- though we were once powerless, we would now have power;

- we would no longer be subject to the law, because we now have grace;
- we would have no fear, because we live by faith; and
- hatred would be substituted with love.

Of course, I could go on and on, but I'll stop here at his love. It was because of his love for you and me that Jesus gave his very life. God loved you and me so much that he manifested himself in human flesh (remember, as John 1 says, the Word was God and the Word was made flesh in Jesus); and then he showed off his miraculous powers and wisdom on the earth, died on the cross, was buried, and then was resurrected.

I just gave a few examples of what Jesus conquered and fulfilled. There are many more. Now I want to also show you a few things God had in mind when he allowed his Son to die for you and me. Through Jesus, we have:

- his divine deliverance—"He personally bore our sins in His [own] body on the tree [as on an altar and offered Himself on it], that we might die (cease to exist) to sin and live to righteousness. By His wounds you have been healed" (1 Peter 2:24 AMP).
- his faith—by faith we understand that the world was framed by the Word of God; so then, faith comes by hearing, and hearing by the Word of God (see Heb. 11:3 and Rom. 10:17).
- his grace—Jesus says, "My grace is sufficient for thee: for my strength is made perfect in weakness" (2 Cor. 12:9).
- his Spirit—"In whom ye also trusted, after that ye heard the word of truth, the gospel of your salvation: in whom also after that ye believed, ye were sealed with that Holy Spirit of promise" (Eph. 1:13).
- his power—"According as his divine power hath given unto us all things that pertain unto life and godliness, through the

knowledge of him that hath called us to glory and virtue" (2 Peter 1:3).

- his promises—"And if ye be Christ's, then are ye Abraham's seed, and heirs according to the promise" (Gal. 3:29).
- his love—"And hope maketh not ashamed; because the love of God is shed abroad in our hearts by the Holy Ghost which is given unto us" (Rom. 5:5).
- his Word—"In the beginning [before all time] was the Word (Christ), and the Word was with God, and the Word was God Himself" (John 1:1 AMP).
- his forgiveness—"If we confess our sins, he is faithful and just to forgive us our sins, and to cleanse us from all unrighteousness" (1 John 1:9).
- his help—"Verily, verily, I say unto you, He that believeth on me, the works that I do shall he do also; and greater works than these shall he do; because I go unto my Father" (John 14:12).
- his blessings—"Blessed be the God and Father of our Lord Jesus Christ, who hath blessed us with all spiritual blessings in heavenly places in Christ" (Eph. 1:3).

The question I have for you is this: why did he die if we don't experience God's love and live in what he left for us? Paul simply puts it like this: "I don't want to frustrate my God by not accepting his grace: for if who I am is by going to church only, then Christ died in vain" (Gal. 2:21, my paraphrase). People of God, accept the precious gift God gave us: his love through Jesus's death on the cross.

God wants you to fully understand this "[that you may really come] to know [practically, through experience for yourselves] the love of Christ, which far surpasses mere knowledge [without experience]; that you may be filled [through all your being] unto all the fullness of God [may have the richest measure of the divine

Presence, and become a body wholly filled and flooded with God Himself]!" (Eph. 3:19 AMP).

This is what Jesus did for you and me. Hallelujah! Christ is in us—we were flooded with him on the inside of us when we gave our life to him. Therefore, we can go before God with boldness knowing God hears our prayers (Eph. 3:12). Because there is one God and one mediator between God and men—that is, Jesus Christ (see 1 Tim. 2:5)—we now have access to God directly, just as Adam and Eve did before they sinned.

The Image of Christ

Who is the image of the invisible God? Jesus. Why did God create man? The answer is in Genesis 1:26–28:

> And God said, Let us make man in our image, after our likeness: and let them have dominion over the fish of the sea, and over the fowl of the air, and over the cattle, and over all the earth, and over every creeping thing that creepeth upon the earth. So God created man in his own image, in the image of God created he him; male and female created he them. And God blessed them, and God said unto them, Be fruitful, and multiply, and replenish the earth, and subdue it: and have dominion over the fish of the sea, and over the fowl of the air, and over every living thing that moveth upon the earth.

I define the *image of God* as the moral and spiritual character of God. When you are in the image of God, people can see a difference in you. They see God in you. I also believe that to be the *likeness of God* is to conduct oneself as God conducts himself—to act like God—by the Spirit of God working through you.

Therefore, it is God's desire that we all conform to the image of Christ. "For those God foreknew he also predestined to be conformed to the likeness of his Son, that he might be the firstborn among many brothers" (Rom. 8:29 NIV).

---

conform: a willingness to act in accordance with or to comply with God's standards, not your own (or anyone else's); to become similar in character and form

---

Being conformed to Christ's image will mean a change in how we relate to others, including—and especially—our spouses. It means that we must be the one who makes the necessary steps toward having a great marriage even when our spouses do not. It means that I am willing to love and to give to my spouse even when they don't deserve it. Our marriages should reflect Jesus's love for the church. Everything God does is motivated by love. Jesus's life exemplified his unconditional love for mankind. He gave his very life for us. I know for sure that you did not go to the depths of hell to fight Satan. Nor were you beaten so badly that people couldn't recognize you. Nor were you mocked with a crown of thorns on your head or nails driven through your hands on a cross. Nor were you buried and resurrected on the third day. Now that is love! God is love, and we are created in his image and likeness. Therefore, the love he freely gave you, you should give to others. The forgiveness he freely gave you, you should give to others. The blessings he freely gave you, you should give to others. Do you get the point?

> Beloved, let us love one another: for love is of God; and every one that loveth is born of God, and knoweth God. He that loveth not knoweth not God; for God is love. In this was manifested the love of God toward us, because that God sent his only begotten Son into the world, that we might live through him. Herein is love, not that we loved God, but that he loved us, and sent his Son to be the propitiation for our sins. Beloved, if God so loved us, we ought also to love one another. No man hath seen God at any time. If we love one another, God dwelleth in us, and his love is perfected in us. Hereby know we that we dwell in him, and he in us, because he hath given us of his Spirit. And we have seen and do testify that the Father sent the Son to be the Saviour of the world. Whosoever shall

confess that Jesus is the Son of God, God dwelleth in him, and he in God. And we have known and believed the love that God hath to us. God is love; and he that dwelleth in love dwelleth in God, and God in him. Herein is our love made perfect, that we may have boldness in the day of judgment: because as he is [love], so are we [love] in this world.

1 John 4:7–17

Jesus is our prime example, and we are to follow and be like him. For example, when we accept Christ in our lives, we become the bride of Christ. We are in him and he in us. Since there is a covenant between you and Christ, when you mess up, you repent (acknowledge wrongdoing and make a commitment to change) and God forgives you. The Bible states that Christ will never leave us nor forsake us. He is committed to his relationship with us. Likewise, in the marriage covenant, we become one with our spouses; therefore, when we have problems or seemingly irreconcilable differences, we should repent and be willing to forgive. We must learn to stay and work out those differences because we are committed to the relationship just like our Savior is committed to us.

Your happiness in your marriage is dependent upon your obedience to God in your thoughts, words, and actions and not dictated by the behavior of your spouse. By obeying the Lord in your daily walk, you show your love for Christ and demonstrate his lordship over your life. Say, for example, that you and your spouse just had a disagreement. You storm out of the house to go to Bible study at church. The Lord tells you to go back into the house and apologize before going to church. You don't want to because you feel that you are right and your spouse is wrong. What do you do?

(a) Go to church without apologizing.
(b) Go back into the house and apologize because God told you to.

God's Word tells us that if you have an argument with a brother, you should leave your offering at the altar, go apologize, and then come back to present your offering (see Matt. 5:23–24). Did you know that your offering could be your praise and worship to him? Guess what: if you have an argument with your spouse and then go to church *without* apologizing, God will not accept your praise and worship. You will have wasted your time. The answer is (b), so go back inside and apologize. Your ego may be bruised a little, but you will demonstrate your love for God by your obedience, and when you get home from church, there will be peace in your home.

God has given us, as born-again believers, all the provisions we need to have a great marriage. I call them the three S's: his Son, his sword, and his Spirit.

1. God has given us his Son, so that we can live a righteous life through him (see 1 John 4:9–10).
2. God has given us his sword (the Bible, the Word of God), which alone will provide specific direction for every area of life (see Eph. 6:17).
3. God has sent his Spirit to dwell in us, to lead us into all truth, to empower us, to help us in times of prayer, and to help us understand the things of God (see John 16:13–14; Rom. 8:26; 1 Cor. 3:16).

In his Word God clearly tells us not to conform to this world but to be transformed by the renewing of our minds (see Rom. 12:2).

> **transform:** to change inwardly. Spiritual transformation means allowing God to be the surgeon; with the help of the Holy Spirit, you undergo a complete makeover in which God's character is developed inwardly while the results are seen outwardly

How do we renew our minds? Ephesians 4:23 says, "And be constantly renewed in the spirit of your mind [having a fresh mental and spiritual attitude]" (AMP).

It is the Word of God that will renew your mind and transform you and your marriage into all that God has called it to be. Below shows you how the Word of God will help you:

- The Word cleanses my mind (see John 15:3).
- The Word sanctifies me or sets me apart (see John 17:17).
- Obeying the Word purifies my soul (see 1 Peter 1:22).

In order to be transformed and conformed into the image and likeness of Christ, you must renew your mind. To be like Christ, we have to:

Act biblically (in thoughts, words, and deeds)

Love biblically (love others unconditionally)

Talk biblically (use the Word as a weapon)

Repent biblically (change our behavior and thoughts)

Unite biblically (become one as husband and wife)

Identify biblically (understand who we are in Christ)

Submit biblically (submit ourselves to others as we would to God)

Minister biblically (live by faith and allow others to experience God through us)

These biblical characteristics form the acronym ALTRUISM, which is the foundation of how we should live as Christians. The more we begin to develop these characteristics, the more we become like Christ.

altruism: a selfless regard or concern for the well-being of others. Caring for others is more important than caring for yourself.

Becoming like Christ is a process. The first step is to believe that you can change from your old ways (the way you think, act, and talk). The second step is to renew your mind by allowing your thoughts to line up with God's Word. Case in point: you may say you believe in divorce. Why? Because the world's system allows divorce. But Moses told the people of Israel that divorce was instituted only because of the hardness of their hearts (selfishness). It was never what God intended. God's Word says he hates divorce (see Mal. 2:16 AMP); therefore you, as a Christian, should hate divorce and never let it become part of your vocabulary. (Note: It is important for each person to develop their own relationship with God so they can understand the Word of God for themselves and do not leave it to anyone else's interpretation. If you are in an abusive situation, search the Bible—God will tell you what to do.)

The final step in becoming like Christ is to be committed to doing what the Word says. You must be willing to submit to God's Word and willing to make the necessary changes in your character. In your obedience, you will be blessed. It has been several years since I began my transformation process, and I am just starting to see the fruit of my labor (the blessing of the Lord) concerning my husband and his transformation. As for me, I am not the same person, and I am very driven to make sure that people will experience God through me, especially my spouse and children.

We now understand how we can be transformed—but *why* should we be transformed? As Christians, our desire should be to seek and please God by learning his ways, his plans, and his purposes for our lives. If you have the desire to fulfill that purpose, you must develop the character of God, which is, simply put, love (see 1 Corinthians 13).

If you are married, you and your spouse should reflect Jesus's unconditional love toward one another. If you do not, you will easily find yourselves part of the skyrocketing divorce statistics. You must make a conscious decision to change. It is no longer acceptable to hide behind the excuse "that is just how I am." We all need to make adjustments in every relationship we enter, whether at work, in our churches, or in our homes. In order to reflect the love of Christ, each spouse has a responsibility to be changed (transformed) into the image of Christ, which is love.

We have been trained by the world that "love is 50–50" or to ask, "What have you done for me lately?" That kind of thinking is selfish and conditional. It is not godly. I thank God that Jesus wasn't selfish and that his love wasn't conditional when he died on the cross for you and me. We have to learn how to love our spouses (and all people, for that matter) unconditionally. This simply means that you love a person because they exist, not because of what they do or do not do for you. The only way you can love unconditionally is to be changed by God through his Word. Furthermore, people in the world need to see and experience the love of God, and that can only be done through believers, the body of Christ. Will you accept today the challenge to be an instrument of love that God can use?

Remember, Jesus gave us all we need to have successful marriages. Let's use all his wisdom and love to develop and nurture the very special gift God gave us: our spouses. Let's honor Jesus's love by demonstrating his love to others, especially our spouses.

Prayer

Thank you, Lord, for showing me areas that I need to work on so that I can display who you are here on the earth. May I decrease right now so that you may increase in me. Continue to perfect me and mold me into your image. Father, continue to show me the areas in my life where I need to be more selfless toward my spouse and my family. I thank you, Lord, that with your help,

I can change. I declare that I am transformed. I make a deliberate decision to do your will and heed what the Spirit of the Lord is telling me. Amen.

For an additional resource, visit the *Marriage 101* website, www.marriage101.us, for a free copy of "The Fruit of Love from A to Z."

ALTRUISM:
Christ's Unconditional Love

Spread love everywhere you go: first of all in your own house. Give love to your wife or husband, to your children, to a next door neighbor. . . . Let no one ever come to you without leaving better and happier. Be the living expression of God's kindness; kindness in your face, kindness in your eyes, kindness in your smile, kindness in your warm greeting.

Mother Teresa

The goal of this section is to help you conform to the image of Christ, which fulfills our created purpose, as seen in Genesis 1:26–28. We were created in God's image and likeness; therefore, our goal should be to be like him. This section will show you the true characteristic of Christ, which is his unconditional love for all mankind. Jesus is the ultimate picture of the definition of *altruism*, which is an unselfish regard for the welfare of others. This section will help you to understand why you were created and how you can be transformed into his image and likeness.

Biblical Example: Jesus and the Church

Jesus had a purpose. He came that all might be saved (see John 16:7). His life was the ultimate example of love and obedience to his Father. His love and obedience allows all those who believe in what he did to be saved from the penalty of sin and eternal death (see Rom. 5:21). His love for us was selfless. He was able to endure the pain and shame of the cross because he saw before him the joy of you and me in right relationship with God (see Heb. 12:2). He is our biblical example of displaying selfless love to others, especially to our spouses.

Ephesians 5:25 states that husbands should love their wives as Christ loves the church and gave himself for it. Verse 33 tells the wife to see to it that she reverences (or respects) her husband. There is no greater love than for a man (or woman) to lay down his (or her) life for another. In the Garden of Gethsemane, Jesus asked God to let the cup of suffering pass from him, but his ultimate statement was, "Nevertheless not as I will, but as thou wilt" (Matt. 26:39). In other words, Jesus was not eager to endure what he was about to endure on the cross, but he realized he had to fulfill his purpose. It was not about him but about God's will.

In marriage, sometimes we may have to say, "Okay, Lord, not my will but yours be done." For example, your spouse may want a family member to move into your house, and you may be totally against it. You pray about it and tell God, "Not my will but yours." Your position of humility and submission allows God to move through you. As you yield to the leading of the Holy Spirit in your relationship with your spouse, you begin to see how this change has a positive impact upon those you come in contact with as they witness God's love moving through you.

Scripture Meditation

Meditate on the following Scriptures, which will show you ways to be transformed into the image of Christ. Ask God to speak to you through them and to reveal to you where you need to change to better reflect these characteristics in your own life. In the space after each verse write down anything God reveals to you.

40

Hebrews 12:1–2 (Message)

"Strip down, start running—and never quit! No extra spiritual fat, no parasitic sins. Keep your eyes on Jesus, who both began and finished this race we're in. Study how he did it. Because he never lost sight of where he was headed—that exhilarating finish in and with God—he could put up with anything along the way: cross, shame, whatever. And now he's there, in the place of honor, right alongside God. When you find yourselves flagging in your faith, go over that story again, item by item, that long litany of hostility he plowed through. That will shoot adrenaline into your souls!"

Galatians 2:20

"I am crucified with Christ: nevertheless I live; yet not I, but Christ liveth in me: and the life which I now live in the flesh I live by the faith of the Son of God, who loved me, and gave himself for me."

Romans 8:4–5 (AMP)

"So that the righteous and just requirement of the Law might be fully met in us who live and move not in the ways of the flesh but in the ways of the Spirit [our lives governed not by the standards and according to the dictates of the flesh, but controlled by the Holy Spirit]. For those who are according to the flesh and are controlled by its unholy desires set their minds on and pursue those things which gratify the flesh, but those who are according to the Spirit and are controlled by the desires of the Spirit set their minds on and seek those things which gratify the [Holy] Spirit."

Ephesians 5:1–2 (Message)

"Watch what God does, and then you do it, like children who learn proper behavior from their parents. Mostly what God does is love you. Keep company with him and learn a life of love. Observe how Christ loved us. His love was not cautious but extravagant. He didn't love in order to get something from us but to give everything of himself to us. Love like that."

Romans 12:1–2 (AMP)

"I appeal to you therefore, brethren, and beg of you in view of [all] the mercies of God, to make a decisive dedication of your bodies [presenting all your members and faculties] as a living sacrifice, holy (devoted, consecrated) and well pleasing to God, which is your reasonable (rational, intelligent) service and spiritual worship. Do not be conformed to this world (this age), [fashioned after and adapted to its external, superficial customs], but be transformed (changed) by the [entire] renewal of your mind [by its new ideals and its new attitude], so that you may prove [for yourselves] what is the good and acceptable and perfect will of God, even the thing which is good and acceptable and perfect [in His sight for you]."

_____

_____

_____

_____

_____

Self-Examination

1. Why did I marry my spouse? (List your reasons.)

2. Do people (including my spouse and children) see Jesus in me—compassion, patience, forgiveness, faithfulness, and obedience to God's Word? If not, what areas do I need to improve?

3. What is missing in my life? In what areas do I feel unfulfilled? Do I look to my spouse for fulfillment? If so, where am I in my relationship with God? How can God help me feel fulfilled in those areas?

4. Am I trying to fix things in my relationship, or do I allow God to fix them? For example, when things are not going the way I think they should, do I tend to make irrational decisions? If my spouse is not changing a behavior I think they should change, do I nag and judge or tell them what they should do?

5. Do I really understand God's perspective on the covenant of marriage? Am I willing to do it his way? Write a prayer to God asking him, "Where do I start?"

Developing Character

Rank the following areas that need improvement in your life, beginning with #1 as the area that needs the greatest improvement, #2 as the next greatest, and so on (see definitions on page 24 to help you).

___ Love
___ Joy
___ Peace
___ Long-suffering
___ Gentleness
___ Goodness
___ Faith
___ Meekness
___ Temperance

Now that you know which areas you need the most work in, focus on the area that needs the greatest improvement until you gain some victory, then start on another. Never take your focus off the previous victory, but continue developing it as you start another. One way to develop each characteristic is to look in a concordance for Scriptures relating to that area, read and meditate on these passages, and allow them to minister to you.

Affirmation

I offer God my life—a living sacrifice. I choose from this day forward to be like Christ, and I am fully committed to being transformed by the renewing of my mind so that I will be changed from the inside out to prove what is the good and perfect will of God for my life.

Reflections

_____

_____

_____

_____

_____

_____

_____

_____

_____

_____

1

Wake Up, Sleeping Beauty!

Marriage Is No Fairy Tale

But refuse profane and old wives' fables, and exercise thyself rather unto godliness. For bodily exercise profiteth little: but godliness is profitable unto all things.

1 Timothy 4:7-8

As I was growing up, I read all the fairy-tale stories like Sleeping Beauty, hoping to one day meet my prince and live happily ever after. Unfortunately, most fairy tales give us an unrealistic picture of what our life with the prince will be like. Cinderella met her prince at a ball, and then he came looking for her with a glass slipper. When he found her, they lived happily ever after—so you too will marry and have a fairy-tale ending, right? That is certainly what I had pictured for my life. You know, "Jewell sees Lewis from afar and is awed by his handsome presence. One day as she is waiting to buy lunch, she turns around and bumps right into her

Prince Charming. They eat together and fall madly in love. They get married and live happily ever after." Well . . . not quite.

Between falling in love and getting married, Lewis and I sought God's guidance and attended an extensive premarital counseling class for three and a half months. The pastor stressed two things that I now know are so important: (1) that couples attend the same church so they are receiving the same teaching and are of the same faith, and (2) that their combined finances are in the black before they get married. He also added that we shouldn't set a date for the wedding before counseling, because people who have done so aren't totally honest with their feelings, especially if they have already put a down payment on a reception area, videographers, and other wedding expenses. After counseling, couples should be one hundred percent sure that they belong together before proceeding into marriage. If you do that, you will be able to weather the storms in your marriage much better when they arise.

And they *will* arise. All couples go through some storms, and your marriage will not be exempt. If you realize this at the beginning, you won't separate or divorce because of false expectations or doubts about whether your spouse is right for you. Instead, when you go through trials and tribulations, you will believe that you are supposed to be with your mate and therefore be willing to do what it takes to make your marriage work. I wish I wasn't giving this advice based on hindsight. I should have given *myself* this advice before our storms came (although I was and still am one hundred percent sure Lewis and I belong together). However, at that time, I just did not know how to get the victory concerning my marriage.

My Storm

I fell in love with a wonderful man. Lewis was literally everything I wanted in a husband. I had written a list of characteristics I wanted in my husband, and I placed this sheet of paper in my Bible and prayed about it. When I met Lewis, I prayed constantly and asked God for confirmation on three different occasions, and God confirmed each time that Lewis was good for me. In fact, the last time, God told me to take out my list and see for myself! Lewis had everything on that list, which consisted of about twenty-five characteristics, except two for which he was seeking God's help. As I'm writing this book sixteen years later, he is actually more than I asked for. Praise God, whose Word is true, for doing exceedingly and abundantly more than what I can ask or think (see Eph. 3:20)!

Lewis and I dated for four years before we got married, and I knew without a shadow of doubt that my marriage was ordained by God. When we went through the storm, I still knew in my heart that Lewis was the man for me, but the devil kept whispering, "You can do better. You don't have to take this." I thought, "I was all right before I met him, and I will be all right when he is gone." My thoughts were stupid. I couldn't do better because I had the best man for me.

We all want the fairy-tale marriage, which is having a perfect man (or woman) without flaws and a perfect life without challenges. That is not reality. Although Lewis is not perfect, he is the perfect person *for me*. And I am not perfect either. I may be a perfectionist, but I am not perfect. I hope you can face that truth about yourself as well, and say it out loud: "I, [fill in your name], am not perfect and neither is [fill in your spouse's name]." Good! Hopefully, confessing it will be a start to a "happily ever after" marriage.

How did Lewis and I go from "perfect for each other" to "I can do better"? When we married in May 1996, we were best friends and got along extremely well. We had some issues and some pet peeves, but the bottom line was that we knew God had put us together for a reason. One month into our marriage, though, we started arguing, and as time went on, the arguments got worse. Sometimes we could go weeks, even months, without arguing, but when we argued, we *argued*. I felt that he wasn't spending enough time with me. He loved to work, and still does, but in my eyes he worked too much. I could have seen this as something great—I had a man who worked hard to take care of his family—but I complained instead. I couldn't see that I was trying to use him as a substitute for something that was missing in my life.

When I got married, I lost practically all my friends. In hindsight, God had separated me from them to draw me closer to him. Therefore, Lewis was the only person I had to talk to or do anything with. I needed him to give me more time because I didn't have anyone else. So my marriage started falling apart right at the beginning because I was looking to Lewis to fulfill me in areas that were now vacant. I eventually learned that God is the only one who can supply all my needs (see Phil. 4:19). If I am unfulfilled, it is not because of my spouse, children, friends, or job. I was putting that weight on Lewis, which was wrong. Psalm 118:8 says, "It is better to trust and take refuge in the Lord than to put confidence in man" (AMP). Now I am not troubled by what Lewis does or doesn't do because my expectation is not in him, but in God. I go to God first, and he will direct Lewis or whomever else to do what is needed for me. As David wrote, "My soul, wait thou only upon God; for my expectation is from him" (Ps. 62:5).

We also argued about finances. Lewis is a saver, and I am a spender. (I am still working on that part!) So he kept his money separate from mine. I started hearing "your money, my money." I used to get so mad because as a couple, it's *our* money. I didn't like him telling me that I couldn't buy the things I wanted (not needed). I worked hard every day. I thought I deserved nice things for myself and my house. Again, my thoughts were out of order. I realize today that if I would have taken my husband's advice concerning finances, we would be stronger financially by now. But I thought he was punishing me.

Then we argued about children. I wanted to adopt first, and Lewis wanted a biological child first. After three years of marriage and not being able to conceive (and after three years of arguing about whose fault that was), he finally agreed to do foster care. We eventually adopted our foster child and afterward conceived our second child. Guess what? Even then, we still argued. We argued about how to raise the kids. I am the disciplinarian parent; he is not. Then there were the arguments that came before and after I became a stay-at-home mom. He could not understand why I needed a break and time to myself.

Many of the arguments we had were simply because we viewed things differently; we had different expectations of one another, finances, raising children, and so on. The issues and challenges we were facing went on and on, and although we continue to deal with issues, we handle them a lot differently than we used to. I seek God as to what I should say or do and whether I should even do anything at all. Now our disagreements and challenges bring us closer to one another instead of dividing us, as they did before.

Selfishness

The biggest challenge you will face in honoring Christ is to change (be transformed into his image and likeness) through doing what his Word says. Biblical change is defined as dying to self and getting rid of selfishness. If you want a marriage that honors God and works the way he designed and created it to, you must be willing to let go of all your selfish desires. Only then will you see his desires for your life and marriage fulfilled.

> **selfish:** concerned only or primarily with oneself without regard for others

Your prayer should be that you are not and never will be selfish—that you will be not a lover of self but a lover of God. It is human nature to be concerned about your own needs, wants, and desires.

51

Christians, however, should be more concerned about the welfare of others. We must seek God on a daily basis to help us turn our attention from being consumed with ourselves to wanting to display Christ outwardly to our spouse and others. Second Timothy 3:2–5 gives a description of those who are "lovers of their own selves" (selfish). Are you the kind of person who focuses on what makes *you* happy and how someone else can please *you* rather than how you can please someone else? If so, then you are probably one of the people that Paul was writing about. In my own life, I see myself as a giver, so I get offended when my husband tells me I am selfish. In my mind, there is no way that I am selfish. But there are times when I *am* selfish, especially with my time and love toward him. There also used to be times when I would get mad at him and not talk to him for days. I wanted to make him suffer because he hurt me. That's selfish.

What many of us see as "selflessness" really isn't. We give what we want to give, to whom we want to give it, and when we want to give it. If someone needs to be loved in a different way than what we are used to, or if someone wants us to do something for them that's inconvenient for us, we don't want to do it. This isn't true selflessness. It's *selfishness*, because we are the ones deciding how, when, and to whom we will give.

Your focus in life should be to please God, not yourself. We must constantly be in a state of pleasing God and being a blessing to others. Below is a list to help you see whether you are self-focused or God-focused:

Self-focused	God-focused
Worry	Belief/trust in God
Fear	Faith
Sin	Righteousness
Selfish	Giving
Natural	Spiritual

Let me provide you with some examples of being self-focused: God has given you a dream or a vision, but you never work toward it because you worry that you can't do it. Or he may have told you to leave a job and go somewhere else, but you're too afraid to leave your comfort zone. He may have told you to stop drinking or smoking or to get out of that adulterous affair, but you continue to do what is pleasing to your flesh. These are all signs that you are self-focused. To be God-focused, you must step out in faith and rely on him because there is no way you can do it without him. It is much easier to be self-focused than it is to follow and trust God. Following God is difficult, and sometimes you will want to quit because it is so hard, just like it is hard to stay in a marriage and work through rough circumstances. But when you get to the other side, there is life and freedom beyond your wildest imagination. God does above and beyond what you can even imagine or think (see Eph. 3:20).

Selfishness, self-centeredness, self-seeking behavior, pride, not forgiving others, and being easily offended are indicators that you are preoccupied with yourself. A focus on self is crippling to your spiritual growth and development and must be turned around if you are to mature in Christ. Always remember the selfless vows you and your spouse made to one another on your wedding day. They were not only your commitment to each other but also your commitment to God. You promised to love and honor one another in sickness and health, for richer and poorer, until death do you part.

Life or Death

I made another mistake in the beginning of my marriage, and it wasn't even a conscious one. It was something I observed from my parents. My mother and father used to play a little game about "Jody," my mother's imaginary boyfriend. When my mother was out all day, my father would always ask her if she had been with Jody, and she would playfully say yes. I brought that game into my marriage, and it caused a lot of confusion and arguments. Lewis even took it a step further. He came up with "Jodette," his pretend girlfriend.

God rebuked me for starting that because we have power to speak life and death into our marriages (see Prov. 18:21). I wasn't speaking life; I was speaking death—adultery. I was just playing, but the devil was waiting to use what I said. Never give the devil a chance to sneak in and seize an opportunity. Lewis and I promised to never speak those names again as long as we live. Make sure you are at all times speaking life into your marriage. Don't say one day, "I love you, baby; you are the best thing that ever happened to me," and the next day tell your spouse, "I hate you! You make me sick, and I wish I never married you!" You just spoke death.

I now think of my mouth as a compass. What comes out of it directs my relationship. For example, if I am going to have a heavenly marriage, I need to speak in that direction, and my actions should support what I am saying. If something is about to come out that would cause my marriage to go south (straight to hell), I don't say it. Anything contrary to the Word of God directs it toward hell. I had to change the direction of my marriage, since it was moving toward adultery. I now confess that my husband wants no one but me, and I don't want anyone but him.

As I've mentioned, once Lewis and I got married, it didn't take long for things to go downhill. We had one argument after another. They started off so small, but the ball kept rolling. Why? Because we never truly sought God's answers to our problems. We didn't seek him concerning how we should communicate or what we should say. God will answer all questions, both small and large. His Word says for us to cast *all our cares* on him (see 1 Peter 5:7). Often we try not to rock the boat, but this leaves trouble unresolved, brewing on the inside and waiting for another opportunity to blow up. However, if we seek God and his answers and handle the problem accordingly, we can resolve the situation without leaving feelings on the inside waiting to erupt. To turn your marriage around, get on your knees and pray for the Lord to direct your mouth, thoughts, and actions. He will give you the wisdom to say just the right thing to turn that problem around. Ever since Lewis and I reconciled, when potential conflicts arise, the Holy Spirit will tell me to just shut up, to apologize even if I am right, or anything else that will stop the argument right in its tracks.

Seeing Beyond the Natural

When Lewis and I got married, I never imagined that we would separate or get a divorce. How did we get to that place of separation? God has since showed me that I was focusing too much on my horizontal relationship with Lewis and not enough on my vertical relationship with my heavenly Father. I was putting too much effort, work, and thought toward changing my husband. I needed to work on myself, praying to the Father and developing a deeper relationship with him. It was not my place, nor my responsibility, to change Lewis—that was God's job. Some of you may be thinking, "I'm not trying to change my spouse." Well, if your spouse is not doing something to your satisfaction, you are trying to change your spouse. I was trying to be God. The Lord, however, told me that he did not need my help. He is God, and he can do all things by himself. I was out of line, out of position, and out of control.

Throughout the whole reconciliation process, I was seeking God with my whole heart, asking question after question. He answered every last one of them. One day the Lord spoke through my pastor and showed me something profound. My pastor said, "We look at our children and spouses in the flesh to the point that we see them as ours." He went on to say that they are ours in the sense that God has blessed us with these individuals; they are a gift from God. But do we own them? No. God owns everything and everyone on this earth (see Ps. 24:1). He bestowed his blessing on us in giving us a spouse and children. Who are we to look at our spouse and children in the natural and not see them as the man, woman, or child God is calling them to be?

---

natural: the attitudes and behaviors you have naturally, which come from your own values, goals, desires, and physical senses (sight, hearing, taste, touch, and smell)

I learned to stop looking at my family in the natural and to start seeing them through the eyes of Christ (spiritually). They may not be where God has called them to be, but you don't know what God has planned for them one, two, five, or ten years from now. I didn't see Lewis beyond what he was in the flesh, so I was focusing on his faults and problems. In 2 Corinthians 5:16 God says, "Consequently, from now on we estimate and regard no one from a [purely] human point of view [in terms of natural standards of value]" (AMP). Bottom line: don't judge your spouse based on what you currently see, but see them from God's perspective. How do you do that? Begin by paying attention to what you say to your spouse. If you hear yourself saying things like, "God wants you to start going to church. God wants you to stop smoking. God wants you to stop going to clubs," then you are looking at the flesh and what your mate is currently doing. The truth of the matter is that you are judging and condemning your spouse, and this does not please God. God is working on that man or woman, and that man is going to become a mighty man of valor or that woman is going to become a virtuous woman in due season. We need to look at our spouses in light of what God has called them to be and the works he is doing through them. We should not go by what we see today, "for we walk by faith, not by sight" (2 Cor. 5:7). The proper view of your mate comes from the Word.

---

spiritual: the attitudes and behaviors you develop as you become sensitive to the Spirit of

---

> God. True spirituality is obeying God in everyday life, being a doer of the Word, and exhibiting God's values, not your own.

So what does God desire men and women of God to be? Believe by faith that he will transform your wife or husband into what the Word of God says about your spouse. It says that he is a man who loves his wife as Christ loves the church (see Eph. 5:25), so your husband will love you that way one day. It says she speaks with wisdom and her husband and children will call her blessed (see Prov. 31:26, 28), so she will be that way one day.

However, that will not happen if you don't continue to pray for and speak those things you desire to see in your mate and marriage (see Mark 11:24). When Lewis and I were going through difficult times in our marriage, all I saw and talked about were negative things. I was looking at all his shortcomings and concentrating more on those negative characteristics than on the positive things that would have shown him as the man of God he is. I believe that if you ask God to reveal to you your man or woman of God, he will open your (spiritual) eyes immediately.

Don't Quit

You may be at a place where you just can't take any more. You may be saying, "I've been with this man for two months (or a year, a couple of years, many years), and *I can't take any more!*" You are ready to throw your marriage away, which means you are ready for separation or divorce. Don't do it. Don't give up! The Bible says, "What *God has joined* together, let man not separate" (Matt. 19:6 NIV, emphasis added). You may have thought you chose your mate. But God has joined the two of you together. Even though you may believe you chose the wrong one, God already knew you were going to marry that particular person, and he can still use your mistakes for his good. God honors all marriages, whether you think you made a mistake or not. God says *no man* (or *woman*) should separate the married couple, and that includes *you*, the one who is about to give up. Don't give up!

In February 2001, my husband and I hit rock bottom after four and a half years of marriage. I hoped a marriage conference would help us, so I asked him to commit to going for the three days. Again, my first mistake was putting my expectation in him and not going to God and having him deal with Lewis's commitment. The first day of the conference, we attended the night session, and I realized that the turnaround in my marriage started with me. I needed to change, and the beauty of it was that I was ready to change. The next day we went to the day sessions, but during the evening session, we literally argued the entire time (quietly, though). I was ready to give up and was tired of arguing with my husband, tired of him not acting right, tired of him not spending time with me and our girls, tired of him not going to church, and tired of him hanging out with the wrong people and doing the wrong things. Just tired of being tired. I didn't feel that we were headed in the same direction. We left the church in separate cars and did not speak to one another at all that evening (we had been sleeping in separate rooms for months already). Lewis left early the next morning, so I assumed he was going to meet me at the church. However, Lewis didn't show up for the day sessions, and I cried throughout the whole service because I was at the end of my rope.

Here I was, hearing God's Word yet feeling so miserable. All I kept hearing at the conference was, "Don't give up!" I kept saying to myself, "It is over." But as I kept listening, I kept hearing God say, "Don't give up!" At the end of those sessions, I told my pastor that the Word was awesome and that what was preached literally changed my life. I was excited about what was going to happen in my marriage as a result of this conference. I went home and Lewis wasn't there so I called him about going to the evening session, and he said he wasn't going.

I would like to think that I am a woman who is filled and controlled by the Holy Spirit, but I lost it. I told him that he had one hour to pack his bags. I now know what it feels like to be temporarily insane. My heart was broken. I was hurting so bad. I thought that if he didn't care about this marriage, I wasn't going to fight for it anymore. I felt that I had been fighting for years already. The main reason we were still together was because I was fighting for our marriage. However, in hindsight I see that I was never fighting. I was nagging, complaining, and judging him. And I was trying to repair a messed-up marriage in my own strength. I was fighting a battle that could only be won by Jesus.

When we are struggling with something, it's probably because we haven't allowed God to help correct the situation. When I completely submitted to the Lord and all he told me to do, I was at peace. I wasn't struggling and wasn't unhappy. Although God had to work on Lewis, and although Lewis may have made my life less peaceful, it didn't faze me. The only thing I was supposed to do was change. It all started with me, and God told me not to worry about Lewis and what he was or was not doing.

When Lewis left on that cold and rainy day to stay in a hotel, the warfare started in my mind. The devil steadily whispered, "You are going to be okay. You were okay before him, and you will be okay after him." But my spirit was saying, "You know what you did was wrong. You know you are supposed to be with this man. This is your husband, the father of your children. You know you were not supposed to throw him out of his house. You are being taught the Word and are supposed to be a doer of the Word. But you are dishonoring the Lord, smacking him in the face, and saying, 'Yes, Lord, I heard your Word, but I just don't want to do what I know is right.'"

I was in even deeper sorrow because I knew that I had hurt my heavenly Father, and I knew better. God told me to fix it. I had to do whatever it took to get Lewis back home because God was not pleased with my actions. God told me to call Lewis that night. Of course, he didn't answer the phone, so I left a message saying that I loved him. That phone call started us toward reconciliation.

So as you can see, I was just like Sleeping Beauty. I had no clue as to what marriage was about or my role in it until Lewis and I separated and I started seeking God for answers. Throughout the reconciliation process, God was showing me his plan and purpose and how my marriage could be "happily ever after"—if I did it his way. Remember, his way is perfect.

Marriage is a lifetime commitment to be dissolved only by death (see Matt. 19:6; Rom. 7:2–3). It takes faith and God's Word to have a great marriage. Victory requires us to be strong and not to quit. Every relationship requires work.

Even though I was very active in church, prayed a lot, and loved the Lord dearly, I was only a hearer of the Word, not a doer. When my husband acted like a fool, I did too. God would tell me to do something nice for Lewis, but since Lewis wasn't being nice to me, I would not act on what I was hearing or reading. But when I went to God and told him I wanted to save my marriage, he said, "Everything I tell you to do, do it."

Once I started developing my relationship with God, I started seeing Lewis in a brand new way. I saw him the way God sees him. For the first time, I began to walk by faith in my marriage and not by sight. I was no longer focused on what Lewis was or was not doing. Rather, my desire was to seek after and pursue God for a closer relationship with him. During this season of my journey, God kept telling me not to quit (get divorced).

Before you decide to move forward with plans to divorce, ask yourself the following questions:

Do I want my marriage?

Have I sought God about what he wants me to do concerning my marriage?

Have I done everything the Lord has instructed me to do concerning my marriage?

Have I sought godly counsel?

Do I have the right attitude concerning my spouse and marriage?

What are the implications if I decide to move forward with divorcing my spouse?

Is there any problem too hard for God to solve in my marriage?

Do I believe God can help me turn my marriage situation around and/or do I want him to?

Acting Biblically

Why should you stay in your marriage? Why should you act biblically even when you feel others don't deserve the results? There are truly tangible benefits to gain in your marriage when you make the decision to govern your life based on the Bible and give up being selfish. For women, the benefit is your ability to win your husband to Christ and cause him to want to change because of the lifestyle that you live. For men, the benefit is to have your wife submit to the godly leadership of the house and to respect the man of God of the house.

Scripture says, "But as he which hath called you is holy, so be ye holy in all manner of conversation" (1 Peter 1:15) and "likewise, ye wives, be in subjection to your own husbands; that, if any obey not the word, they also may without the word be won by the conversation of the wives" (1 Peter 3:1). In these two Scriptures, "conversation" is not defined by what you say. It is defined by what you do—your conduct and manner of living.

Although the second Scripture refers to the wife, the first Scripture is for all Christians, both men and women. You have the ability to make an impact upon your spouse (and anyone else) by introducing them to Jesus through your godly lifestyle and behavior. If your spouse doesn't go to church and you do, ask yourself: Can my spouse see a difference between me and him? Am I the same person I was prior to getting saved—still cursing, still being mean and nasty, or still nagging and being judgmental? Can my spouse see a change in me? Even if he (or she) is mean and nasty, am I willing to show love? If the answer to that last question is yes, then you are a person who has overcome being consumed with their own selfish concerns and who is *acting biblically*, according to God's Word.

Let me give you an example of acting biblically. A famous argument in our home centered around Lewis's expectations of me cooking dinner. Lewis wants a freshly prepared meal daily. To relieve the burden on me, I sometimes cooked a lot so we could have leftovers. One day we had a big argument because he threw away the leftovers, so we had nothing for the following day. The argument got very heated, and he walked out, slamming the door. Of course, the first voice I heard was the Spirit of God, telling me to call Lewis to apologize and ask what he would like for dinner. My flesh was screaming, "No way! I will have bread and water waiting for him when he gets home!" But after a few minutes, I did what God said, and then I fixed a freshly prepared meal with joy (okay, just a little joy). Acting biblically is more than just what you intend to do; it's what you actually do. It's doing what God tells you to do even when you don't want to. Therefore, acting biblically is doing what is right. That is probably where we got the phrase "What would Jesus do?" As Christians we must ever be mindful of what Jesus would do. Again, it is not what you say but how you act—your consistent godly behavior—that will win souls and your spouse.

Prayer

Father, in the name of Jesus, I ask for your help so that I may change. Create in me a clean heart and renew a right spirit in me. Thank you that my steps are ordered by you; therefore, I can be and do all you ask me to. Thank you that as I am working on this exercise, my ears are open to hear from you, my mind is alert, and my heart is prepared to hear and do what the Spirit of the Lord is telling me to do. I desire to be unselfish. I yield my mind, body, and soul to you as a living sacrifice so I may be and do your good pleasure. Father, help me to not operate in strife or selfishness toward my spouse and others. Instead, in the true spirit of humility, let me esteem my spouse and others as more important than myself. I can run this race with patience, knowing there is a joy set before me—a "happily ever after" marriage. In Jesus's name, amen.

For more on this topic, visit www.marriage101.us to receive the article "Are You Selfish?"

ALTRUISM:
Act Biblically

The goal of this section is to help you realign your priorities so that you *act biblically*. You may think you are already acting biblically, but ask yourself: Is my marriage reflective of Jesus's love, which is a selfless and unconditional love? Or is my love conditional? Are my acts of kindness based on how my spouse treats me? Marriage is sacred and beautiful, yet it requires work and God's help. In order for it to be successful, someone needs to start the reconciliation process—and that someone is you. To aid you in this process, this workbook section is designed to help you examine yourself and get rid of everything in your heart that is not pleasing to God. This includes selfishness. This section is designed to help you learn to act, talk, and think differently concerning your marriage. You should expect to see immediate improvements in your marriage following your decision to *act biblically*.

Biblical Example: Adam and Eve (Genesis 2–3)

Adam and Eve are the very first married couple in the Bible. They are the one couple whose marriage had all of the essential components for success: oneness, a great personal relationship with God,

65

a beautiful garden to call home (all except one tree, the tree of the knowledge of good and evil), and no one there to tempt them except the serpent, who tempted them with the only thing they really had, which was a word from God. God had given them the authority to rule the world, but they gave this authority to the serpent when he persuaded them to eat a piece of fruit that looked good but that God had specifically told them not to eat. The world was cursed because of this one act of disobedience.

God has given you, just like Adam and Eve, everything you need and desire in your mate. Don't let the selfish act of adultery or any other sin take your eyes off God.

Some boundaries are necessary for you to have an intimate and personal relationship with God and your spouse. The first is that, in order to have that kind of relationship, you must be obedient to God's Word. The other is that you eat fruit (enjoy sexual intimacy) from your own tree and not from another. God's Word gives us freedom, but in that freedom is a responsibility to act on the word we hear. Jesus died so that we could have the same kind of relationship Adam and Eve had with God in the beginning. We can now have that intimate personal relationship with God and with one another by aligning our thoughts and actions to the will of God *through* the Word of God.

Scripture Meditation

Meditate on the following Scriptures, which will show you whether or not you are acting biblically. Ask God to speak to you through these Scriptures and reveal to you what behavior you need to change so that you can be transformed. Write down anything God reveals to you in the space after each verse.

2 Corinthians 13:5–6 (AMP)

"Examine and test and evaluate your own selves to see whether you are holding to your faith and showing the proper fruits of it. Test and prove yourselves [not Christ]. Do you not yourselves realize and know [thoroughly by an ever-increasing experience] that Jesus Christ is in you—unless you are [counterfeits] disapproved on trial and rejected? But I hope you will recognize and know that we are not disapproved on trial and rejected."

_____

_____

_____

_____

_____

1 Peter 2:20 (Message)

"There's no particular virtue in accepting punishment that you well deserve. But if you're treated badly for good behavior and continue in spite of it to be a good servant, that is what counts with God."

_____

_____

_____

_____

_____

2 Timothy 3:2–5 (AMP)

"For people will be lovers of self and [utterly] self-centered, lovers of money and aroused by an inordinate [greedy] desire for wealth, proud and arrogant and contemptuous boasters. They will be abusive (blasphemous, scoffing), disobedient to parents, ungrateful, unholy and profane. [They will be] without natural [human] affection (callous and inhuman), relentless (admitting of no truce or appeasement); [they will be] slanderers (false accusers, troublemakers), intemperate and loose in morals and conduct, uncontrolled and fierce, haters of good. [They will be] treacherous [betrayers], rash, [and] inflated with self-conceit. [They will be] lovers of sensual pleasures and vain amusements more than and rather than lovers of God. For [although] they hold a form of piety (true religion), they deny and reject and are strangers to the power of it [their conduct belies the genuineness of their profession]."

Colossians 3:8–10, 12–17

"But now ye also put off all these; anger, wrath, malice, blasphemy, filthy communication out of your mouth. Lie not one to another, seeing that ye have put off the old man with his deeds; And have put on the new man, which is renewed in knowledge after the image of him that created him. . . . Put on therefore, as the elect of God, holy and beloved, bowels of mercies, kindness, humbleness of mind, meekness, longsuffering; Forbearing one another, and forgiving one another, if any man have a quarrel against any: even as Christ forgave you, so also do ye. And above all these things put on charity, which is the bond of perfectness. And let the peace of God rule in your hearts, to the which also ye are called in one body; and be ye thankful. Let the word of Christ dwell in you richly in all wisdom; teaching and admonishing one another in psalms and hymns and spiritual songs, singing with grace in your hearts to the Lord. And whatsoever ye do in word or deed, do all in the name of the Lord Jesus, giving thanks to God and the Father by him."

_____

_____

_____

Colossians 3:12 (AMP)

"Clothe yourselves therefore, as God's own chosen ones (His own picked representatives), [who are] purified and holy and well-beloved [by God Himself, by putting on behavior marked by] tenderhearted pity and mercy, kind feeling, a lowly opinion of yourselves, gentle ways, [and] patience [which is tireless and long-suffering, and has the power to endure whatever comes, with good temper]."

_____

_____

_____

_____

_____

Self-Examination

1. Is my relationship with my spouse selfish? In what ways? (List them.)

2. In what ways can I give more of myself to my mate?

3. What are some things that I have been told or have come to believe prior to my marriage that I need to remove from my mind?

4. What are some things my spouse does or doesn't do that I think are hindering us in some way? What are some things *I* am doing or not doing that don't help the marriage? (Write them all down and then compare your list of flaws to your spouse's. His (or her) flaws don't look so bad now, do they?)

5. What behavioral changes do I need to make? For example, have I been holding out on sex or throwing things at my spouse because I am mad at him (or her)? Have I been leaving the house for hours without checking in? Do I have a lack of patience?

Developing Character

Make a decision to examine and correct your selfish ways this week. When you notice a selfish act, find ways to sacrifice your desires in order to help your spouse and improve your relationship. This exercise will help you in developing the godly character of *acting biblically*. Trust me, the Holy Spirit will reveal to you the areas where you need to make corrections—if you have ears to hear.

Affirmation

I will obey God's commandments because I trust him, and I will reap his rewards.

Reflections

_____

_____

_____
_____
_____
_____
_____
_____
_____
_____
_____
_____
_____
_____
_____
_____
_____
_____
_____
_____
_____
_____
_____
_____

2

The Good Fairy

The Holy Spirit Is Our Helper

But the Comforter, which is the Holy Ghost, whom the Father will send in my name, he shall teach you all things, and bring all things to your remembrance, whatsoever I have said unto you.

John 14:26

In the Sleeping Beauty story, the good fairies had magical powers and pronounced blessings over the princess. God, of course, is not a magician, but he gave us the Holy Spirit, who guides us and directs us into all truth. God has given us certain roles in life, and in his Word he explains how we should fulfill them. It is important that we, as Christians, understand God's plan for our individual roles and that we identify with those prescribed roles so that we can function in them accordingly. The Holy Spirit helps us to carry out God's plan and purpose for our lives when we rely upon him. So why is it so difficult for us to do what he says concerning our

73

marriage and any other area we may be struggling in? Maybe it is because we have our own ideas and purposes that are not in line with God's.

Singleness

I hope some people will read this book *before* they get married, not just when their marriage is in trouble. So before I talk more about marriage, I want to deal with singleness.

> **singleness:** time set aside to seek the Lord for his will and purpose for your life

Genesis 1:27 says, "God created man in his image . . . male and female created he them." We need to understand God's plan as far as order. He knew from the beginning that he was going to create male and female. God created everything else in the world before he made the "very good" thing: man (Gen. 1:31). Man was made to take care of, and be in charge of, all that was created. Therefore, God put him in a position (job) first. Adam's job was to name all the animals and till the ground.

Women, there is a reason men take so long to ask for your hand in marriage. Men need to get things in order (career, education, and finances) before they take on the responsibility of a wife. So where did men get this way of thinking? They got it from Adam. God made Adam first, to get things prepared before Eve came. That is why she is a "helpmeet": she helps him in his job. Women, if you are not willing to change your life and your plans by submitting to your man of God and his plans, don't get married. Being single means you can do what you want when you want. If you have goals you want to achieve, do them now. Also use this time to develop a deeper relationship with God. God wants you, at this stage, to become fulfilled and happy in him so that when you do get married, you don't have to seek fulfillment from your mate because you already bring it into the marriage.

Another reason a man may take awhile to get married is that he is not ready to leave his mama. As the Bible says, "Therefore shall a man leave his father and his mother, and shall cleave unto his wife" (Gen. 2:24). Deciding to marry is a big step for a man to take. It means he becomes totally responsible for another human being. When Adam and Eve ate from the forbidden tree, they both were in trouble, but Adam took more of the punishment because he was responsible for his wife. In Genesis 3:11, God said to Adam, "Who told you that you were naked? Have you eaten from the tree that I commanded you not to eat from?" (NIV). In verse 17, God told Adam, "Because you listened to your wife and ate from the tree . . . cursed is the ground because of you; through painful toil you will eat of it all the days of your life" (NIV). Praise God that we are no longer under the curse because of Jesus's death!

As a single person, you should spend your extra time developing an intimate relationship with God. Developing that relationship prior to marriage will help you become a mature, loving, and whole person, which is very important to having a successful marital relationship. It is during your season of singleness that if you allow God to guide your path (to your career, education, ministry, and spouse), then he will unfold his plan and purpose for your life. It is during this time that you are building a spiritual foundation that will help you in the years to come.

The Bible says that before their fall into sin, Adam and Eve were both naked and were not ashamed (see Gen. 2:25). To me, that describes the core of the word *intimacy*. They saw each other as God saw them (and later, because of sin, they saw each other in the flesh and covered themselves in shame). When you are in genuine intimacy with someone, you are not trying to change them. You see and accept them for who they are. You are not ashamed of who they are or what they do. And you can show yourself to that person at your weakest point and not fear that they will use it against you. This is a place of genuine intimacy that couples should strive toward in their marriage.

When I was in the hospital for four months, I was totally bedridden. I couldn't even get up to go to the bathroom or take a shower. I was completely in the hands of the nurses and Lewis. I believe that experience was the most intimate yet grueling time in our marriage. My husband took care of me like no other person in this world would ever do. It wasn't a time for me to be embarrassed or ashamed. However, before that, there were things that I wouldn't do because I was embarrassed. My husband never saw the real me until then and probably never would have if not for that circumstance.

Intimacy is more than sex; it is a deep inner connection—souls are connected when you are not ashamed. So don't hide your deepest secrets and fears from your potential mates. Let them see what your weaknesses are so they can cover them when crises arise. If you find that you are not able to be "naked" and unashamed with your potential future spouse, ask God to reveal the reason and then work together as a couple to achieve the level of intimacy necessary to have a successful, fulfilling marriage. If your struggle with intimacy is caused by something that happened prior to meeting this person, please seek wise counsel to help you work through the issue to become that whole person that God desires you to be in your marriage.

Shame is a big part of many couples' struggles to achieve an intimate relationship. We can put on an act and lie to each other because we are ashamed of who we are. We go into relationships fearing that the person we love won't love us if he or she knows our past secrets. Guess what? When we do this, we are already in the hands of Satan. If you don't open up to your potential mate now, then later on you will be wondering why you are having so many problems in your marriage. The devil will use that as an opportunity to destroy your marriage. For those who are not yet married, this is a perfect opportunity to show your worst as well as your best side.

If the person stays with you when you are at your worst, then he or she will be there always.

Marriage is work. It is probably the hardest yet most rewarding thing you will ever do. My husband told me that on our wedding day his brother (who was already married) told him that this could be the best thing or the worst thing he would ever do. I was told that both of them were in the back room crying like babies for half an hour while I was waiting and wondering why the wedding hadn't started. But Lewis's brother was right. You can have a great marriage or a really bad marriage. The choice is yours! A great marriage is going to take a lot of work and prayer. If you are not willing to put the work into having a long-lasting, until-death-do-you-part marriage, you do not need to get married at this time.

The Role of the Husband

A husband is to (1) be head of their household, (2) honor his wife, and (3) love his wife. To love your wife as Christ loves the church (see Eph. 5:25) is simply to lay down your life for her. It is the husband's responsibility to make sure his wife and children have what they need.

First Corinthians 11:3 says, "Now I want you to realize that the head of every man is Christ, and the head of the woman is man, and the head of Christ is God" (NIV). However, the word *head* indicates responsibility and accountability. Being the head does not mean superiority, nor does it give a right to be dictatorial or demanding. When a couple cannot reach a decision together, the man should make the final decision. Men, women are looking to you to lead them in truth by the Word of God. Men, you are subject to authority as well—you are held accountable to Christ for your actions, words, thoughts, and behavior toward your wife and others.

And men, in case you didn't know, you are also to submit to your wife (see Eph. 5:21). You may ask, "Why do I submit to her?" You must submit out of reverence for Christ. See her as a woman of God who is like Christ on the earth, and treat her and talk to her as if Christ were in the room with you. Honor her by treating her with consideration and respect on the basis of shared faith. The apostle Paul counseled:

> Husbands, love your wives, as Christ loved the church and gave Himself up for her, so that He might sanctify her, having cleansed her by the washing of water with the Word, that He might present the church to Himself in glorious splendor without spot or wrinkle or any such things [that she might be holy and faultless]. Even so husbands should love their wives as [being in a sense] their own bodies. He who loves his own wife loves himself.
>
> Ephesians 5:25–28 AMP

How should you love your wife? Verse 29 says to nourish (to foster the development of) and carefully protect and cherish her. Men, you will read other things throughout this book that you must do. But for now, know that you are ultimately responsible and held accountable for your family. Therefore, if nothing else, the man of God must know the Word of God.

A Man after God's Own Heart

God sent Samuel to tell King Saul that he was being replaced. "And Samuel said to Saul, 'You have done foolishly. You have not kept the commandment of the LORD your God, which He commanded you. For now the LORD would have established your kingdom over Israel forever. But now your kingdom shall not continue. The LORD has sought for Himself a man after His own heart [David]'" (1 Sam. 13:13–14 NKJV). Although King David committed adultery and was a murderer, he was a man after God's own heart. Why? Because he repented (acknowledged wrongdoing and made a commitment to change) and did what God was telling him to do. Acts 13:22 in the Amplified Bible defines a man after God's own heart as one who will do all of God's will and carry out God's plan fully. Even though David had to suffer the consequences of his sin, his love for God never failed—he ran toward God, not from him. As a man, especially a husband, your goal should be to become a man after God's own heart.

God told Samuel to go anoint one of Jesse's sons to be king. Samuel's first thought was to anoint the eldest son. "But the Lord said to Samuel, Look not on his appearance or at the height of his stature. . . . For the Lord sees not as man sees; for man looks on the outward appearance, but the Lord looks on the heart" (1 Sam. 16:7 AMP). What is God looking for in his people? He is looking for those who have a heart to carry out his plan here on earth. Acts 13:22 says, "He raised up David to be their king; of him He bore witness and said, I have found David, the son of Jesse a man after My own heart, who will do all My will and carry out My program fully" (AMP). As we saw with Saul, the Lord rejects those who do not obey his commandments, but he seeks after those who are willing and obedient to carry out his will.

Does this mean that you are without sin if you are a man after God's own heart? No, we all sin and fall short of the glory of God (see Rom. 3:23). God loved David even though he had some weaknesses (women and pride) and sin (adultery and murder). But David is known and admired for his leadership. To list just a few of his godly qualities: David was a man of patience (he was anointed but waited for his time to be king), was a man of courage (fought against a Philistine giant), was honorable (kept his commitment to Jonathan and his family), was humble (quickly repented and asked for forgiveness), and had a personal relationship with God (prayed and obeyed God). David fulfilled what he was called to do: becoming king over Israel, bringing the ark of the covenant back to Jerusalem, and leading armies to victory in the conquest of the Promised Land. He finally understood why he was king and his lineage was so blessed: David realized why the Lord had made him king—it was because God wanted to pour out his kindness on Israel. God's kindness was Jesus, who is from the lineage of King David.

All who have accepted God's kindness can continue to receive his blessings because we are a chosen generation (see 1 Peter 2:9). As a leader in your community, in your job, in your church, and definitely in your home, how do you influence those around you? Are you admired for your leadership abilities? Ask God to show you how to be a godly leader whom he can use.

The Role of a Wife

A wife has three important responsibilities: (1) submit to her own husband (hereafter referred to as her "man of God"), (2) reverence her man of God, and (3) be a helpmeet to her man of God.

What does being a "helpmeet" mean? She *helps* him fulfill the call that God has predestined for his life. Does she also have a predestined call on her life? Absolutely! Being a helpmeet to your husband does not take away from who you are as a woman or what God is calling you to do. Being a helpmeet is not a state of helplessness but a state of helping, a supporting role. Although the husband is the leader, both of us have dominion. The Bible says, "And God said, Let us make man in our image, after our likeness: and let them have dominion over . . . all the earth. . . . So God created man in his own image, in the image of God created he him; male and female created he them. And God blessed them, and God said unto them, Be fruitful, and multiply, and replenish the earth, and subdue it: and have dominion over . . . every living thing that moveth upon the earth" (Gen. 1:26–28). As you can see, men *and* women are called to have dominion, yet in different roles. Your husband may have been called to a ministry position, and your role may be to help him fulfill that role. Believe me, in that role you will either find who you are or learn some valuable lessons about yourself.

God knows all things, and he knew the union that would take place between you and your spouse and how he could use it for his glory. He made sure that the woman would be fit and able to help

80

her husband be and do all that God is calling him to be and do. He made the man more than able to be a man of God in a place of authority over his family, to lead his wife and children to fulfill the will of God for *their* lives. Conflict arises in our relationships when we work outside of our God-given roles. For example, a woman was created by God to be a helper or an assistant to her husband. Therefore, when she tries to be the head of the family within that marital relationship, problems arise. Why? Because she is functioning outside of the role God created for her. Functioning within your role as a wife can be very difficult, especially when it comes to submission. Remember, there is grace a wife can receive, through prayer, when she needs help. In 2 Corinthians 12:9, Paul relates the profound truth, "[God] said unto me, My grace is sufficient for thee: for my strength is made perfect in weakness." Paul also stated that he would all the more glory in his weakness (persecutions, infirmities, hardships, insults, and difficulties), knowing that the strength of Christ would rest upon him. When we admit our reluctance (our unwillingness to sacrifice our own wants and desires), we allow God's strength to take over.

God wants women to meditate on 1 Peter 3:1–6. If you read this by the leading of the Holy Spirit, you will understand that to do this is to walk before God with a pure heart and be a woman after God's own heart. In the Amplified version, it says:

> In like manner, you married women, be submissive to your own husbands [subordinate yourselves as being secondary to and dependent on them, and adapt yourselves to them], so that even if any do not obey the Word [of God], they may be won over not by discussion but by the [godly] lives of their wives, when they observe the pure and modest way in which you conduct yourselves, together with your reverence [for your husband; you are to feel for him all that reverence includes: to respect, defer to, revere him—to honor, esteem, appreciate, prize, and, in the human sense, to adore him, that is, to admire, praise, be devoted to, deeply love, and enjoy your husband]. Let not

yours be the [merely] external adorning with [elaborate] interweaving and knotting of the hair, the wearing of jewelry, or changes of clothes; but let it be the inward adorning and beauty of the hidden person of the heart, with the incorruptible and unfading charm of a gentle and peaceful spirit, which [is not anxious or wrought up, but] is very precious in the sight of God. For it was thus that the pious women of old who hoped in God were [accustomed] to beautify themselves and were submissive to their husbands [adapting themselves to them as themselves secondary and dependent upon them].

I must interject here: ladies, it is important that we forget what we have been taught about being independent and not depending on anyone. That is not God's way. You can still be who God has called you to be while obeying the Word of God. First Corinthians 11:11 says, "Nevertheless, in [the plan of] the Lord and from His point of view woman is not apart from and independent of man, nor is man aloof from and independent of woman" (AMP). I wasn't programmed biblically when I got married. My independence made my husband feel as though I really didn't need him. It got so bad that I started to think I really didn't—until he was gone. I've learned and now realized that it is very important for men to feel needed. That's what reverencing our husbands accomplishes.

Continuing in 1 Peter we read:

It was thus that Sarah obeyed Abraham [following his guidance and acknowledging his headship over her by] calling him lord [master, leader, authority]. And you are now her true daughters if you do right and let nothing terrify you [not giving way to hysterical fears or letting anxieties unnerve you].

1 Peter 3:6 AMP

I like the way this Scripture ends by emphasizing that you are con-sidered a true daughter of Sarah if you don't allow fear and anxieties stop you from doing the right thing toward your husband. Fear is a roadblock that stops women from reverencing their husbands in the way that Sarah did. Godly reverence for your husband is what God expects from us as wives. If you are feeling any anxiety about acknowledging your husband's role as "head" or "leader" over you or the family because of fear that he may take advantage of you in some way, seek the Scriptures on overcoming fear and ask the Lord to assist you in taking steps in this area of your marriage.

Reverencing our husbands is so important. I remember one day when Lewis and I were talking. I wasn't paying him much attention, and he threw out how I listen so attentively to my pastor, hanging on to every word that he preaches, and yet I can't seem to listen to him with the same attentiveness. Though his work may sometimes seem boring to me, I need to listen. Listening is another way we can reverence our husbands. We can also let them know how important they are and how much we and our children really need them. When Lewis walks through the door, our girls get so excited, screaming, "Daddy!" and jumping up and down. Sometimes I do the same thing! I know it makes his hard day great to have all his girls light up like Christmas trees when he walks in the door.

Here are some other ideas to make your man of God feel special: Fix him a candlelight dinner or breakfast in bed. Read between the lines and help him with something even though he didn't ask (taking out the trash or mowing the lawn). Call him up and ask, "What does my man of God want for dinner?" These are just little ways we can reverence our husbands. At a mom's meeting, one lady said that her husband likes having a pedicure. That is so awesome. If Jesus could wash his disciples' feet, surely we can wash our husbands' feet!

Proverbs 31 shows us the type of woman we should emulate. Maybe you have read Proverbs 31 a million times. But every time we read it, we should get a new revelation. Wherever we are in life, it will apply. When I read it for the first time, I read it from a wife's perspective. When my husband asked me to leave my career and become a stay-at-home mom, I read it from a home-maker's viewpoint. As I was contemplating whether to start a home-based business, I read it from a businesswoman's point of view. And when I started seeking God more diligently, I read it simply as a woman of God. So this one passage applies in a lot of different ways.

As women of God, we need to strive to be virtuous women. We need to be guided and directed by the Word of God. As Christian women filled with the Holy Spirit, we need to be controlled by the Holy Spirit at all times. Therefore, our reserve of the Word of God should never run low. God says that his people perish because they lack knowledge (see Hosea 4:6). Being filled with the Word helps us to be all that God has called us to be, whether we are a spouse, an employee, or a friend.

Moreover, women, keep your tongue under control. I know that my tongue used to be lethal. I would say things that I knew would hurt my husband or anyone else. But Proverbs 31 says that when I open my mouth, the law of kindness should be on my tongue (see v. 26). When each of us decided to accept Jesus into our lives, we also accepted the responsibilities that go with that. Therefore, we must read the Word and do what it says. Our responsibility to God is to show him on the earth. God is love, and there is no evil in him. Therefore, honor him in every word you speak.

In summary, the wife's role is that of an enabler, a cheerleader, and a helper. She should be trustworthy and dependable while edifying and building up her husband at all times.

Virtuous Women

Proverbs 31 talks of all the qualities of a virtuous woman. One verse states that "her children arise up, and call her blessed; her husband also, and he praiseth her" (v. 28). Our men of God should be calling us blessed and praising us. Is your husband calling you blessed? Does he praise you? If not, is there something you are not doing that you should be? Ask God—he will show you the areas where you need to make some improvements in your role as wife and mother and in all the other roles you play.

In the book of Ruth, Ruth's fiancé, Boaz, told her that his whole city knew that she was a virtuous woman (see Ruth 3:11). Why was she virtuous? Ruth was a Moabite (and, research says, a king's daughter). She was married to one of Naomi's sons for about ten years. When Ruth's husband and brother-in-law died, her mother-in-law (Naomi) wanted to return to her people, the Israelites. Naomi tried to get Ruth and her sister-in-law to stay with their own people and their own gods, but Ruth insisted on going with Naomi. When Ruth's husband died, she had no reason to leave Moab. Yet she left because in her eyes she was no longer a Moabite. She was an Israelite who took on her husband's name and all that came with it. "And Ruth said, Urge me not to leave you or to turn back from following you; for where you go I will go, and where you lodge I will lodge. Your people shall be my people and your God my God" (Ruth 1:16 AMP).

I received a lot of insight from reading this book in the Bible. First, Ruth's mother-in-law was a woman of God. Ruth saw God in Naomi; that is why she wanted to follow her and her God. Second, she gave herself to her husband completely in name, heritage, religion, and spirit. Again, she was no longer a king's daughter or a Moabite. How many of us have kept our maiden names because we thought we would lose our identity? When you follow God's way of doing things, you don't lose anything; you gain. Once in Bethlehem, Ruth immediately went out to work because they were not well off. Just think of the attitude most of us would have if we were in her shoes. In fact, let's bring it closer to home. Say your husband wants to start a janitorial service and wants you to come work for him. Would you think that kind of work was beneath you? Or try this one: you have a graduate degree, a career you love, and a very nice salary, but your husband wants you to leave your career to take care of the children and home. What would you say? "How dare you ask me to be a stay-at-home mom!" Oops, that one hurt! That is exactly what happened to me. However, I've learned to trust God and my man of God. I encourage you to do the same.

Our identity comes from recognizing who we are in Christ and what God is calling us to do for him in whatever state we are in (see 1 Cor. 7:20). To be a stay-at-home mom is a calling. Whether you are married or single, helping your spouse to fulfill his call or just fulfilling what you are required to do, both are special callings from God. As a Christian, you should use whatever state you are in and your gifts to serve God and the people that he has entrusted to you.

Before I wrote this book, outside influences (everything aside from the Bible) helped me develop my image as a wife and as a person. I thought I had to have my own bank account, be my own person, and depend on no one. This, of course, brought on lots of arguments with my husband. It wasn't until we separated that I started seeking God's advice as to my role as a wife. I had to be willing to let go of what I was taught and implement what God was telling me. His Word has helped me to realize who I am as a wife without losing who I am as a person.

---

identify: to associate or affiliate oneself closely with a person or group

---

Becoming a woman of God has helped me to become a better wife and a better mother and has definitely shown me my purpose, which was very important to me because I have always desired to do great things for God. Through studying the Scriptures, I've realized that I had to lose who I thought I was to become who I am today in Christ. Matthew 16:25 says, "For whosoever will save his life shall lose it: and whosoever will lose his life for my sake shall find it." Throughout life, seek God's plan and not your own. After leaving a twelve-year career, I realized that it was all part of God's plan for me to be where I am today. Because Ruth followed her mother-in-law, she ended up marrying a wealthy man and having a son who became the grandfather of David, the ancestor of Jesus.

Ruth is the only woman in the Bible called a virtuous woman. I believe it was because she took on the identity of her husband and followed after the things of God. For example, if you belong to the Jehovah's Witnesses and you marry a Christian, you need to take on your husband's identity, Christianity. If you look at this as a loss, you may hold up what God has for you. The reasons why women should take on their husband's identity are: (1) your children's heritage comes from the father, (2) you need to honor your husband, and (3) so you can receive all that God has for you (or, to put it another way, because it is his will). If your husband is an unbeliever, then you should pray for your spouse and lead by example. Moreover, read 1 Corinthians 7:11–15, which shows that an unbeliever is sanctified by the spouse who is a believer. There is hope if you believe in the Word of God: "For surely there is a latter end [a future and a reward], and your hope and expectation shall not be cut off" (Prov. 23:18 AMP). My husband has made remarkable changes and has grown so much spiritually because of the changes I made. While some think I am crazy, others have called me blessed, including my husband. Therefore, I am becoming what the Bible calls "a virtuous woman."

Marriage

What is marriage?

> **marriage:** a divine institution created by God in which two completely different people (male and female) have chosen to enter into a covenant relationship to make a lifetime commitment to God and to one another that they will stay with their imperfect spouses and love one another as God loves them—unconditionally

In marriage the two shall become one—two different individuals with vast differences and goals have agreed to come together as one. They have shared desires, goals, dreams, and plans, and they are connected spiritually. Marriage is a covenant (a pledge, vow, promise, or agreement made between two parties to carry out the terms agreed upon). It cannot—or should not—be terminated until the death of a spouse. Therefore, when you got married, you made a covenant commitment to God that you would do the words you spoke and that you would let him have his way in your marriage; it is *his* institution, after all. Psalm 89:34 states, "My covenant will I not break, nor alter the thing that is gone out of my lips." If you want God's blessing, you must remain faithful to him. If you don't, your offerings (such as praise and worship, tithes and offerings, blessings and honor, and your seeking of forgiveness) may be rejected. Keep this in perspective. Although God is a loving and forgiving God, you cannot go before him with your offerings without having repented for how you've been treating your spouse or for not having changed your ways.

As the prophet Malachi said of our offerings:

> Yet you ask, Why does He reject it? Because the Lord was witness [to the covenant made at your marriage] between you and the wife of your youth, against whom you have dealt treacherously and to whom you were faithless. Yet she is your companion and the wife of your covenant [made by your marriage vows]. And did not God make [you and your wife] one [flesh]? Did not One make you and preserve your spirit alive? And why [did God make you two] one? Because He sought a godly offspring [from your union]. Therefore take heed to yourselves, and let no one deal treacherously and be faithless to the wife of his youth. For the Lord, the God of Israel, says: I hate divorce and marital separation and him who covers his garment [his wife] with violence.
>
> Malachi 2:14–16 AMP

Some problems in our relationships may come from poor self-image or low self-esteem. Many of us have listened to others who have told us who *they* think we are. And yet we have not understood what Christ did for us. Therefore, not knowing who we are in Christ and what we have in him, we see ourselves through the eyes of others. This can create all sorts of problems. For example, if you let your spouse abuse you, people may tell you that you have a low self-image. In reality, you may stay with your spouse either because you truly love him or because you're afraid to leave because of what he may do to you or a family member. I don't believe you have a low self-image. You simply don't know what the Word says about that situation and do not understand who you are in Christ. God's Word says that God does not give us the spirit of fear but of love, power, and a sound mind (see 2 Tim. 1:7) and that even though God hates divorce, he also hates violence in marriage (see Mal. 2:16). Therefore, seek God concerning your situation and hear from him what you should do.

Please note that a proper view of self comes from an understanding of who we are in Christ (see Rom. 8:14–17; Eph. 1:3–14; 1 Peter 2:9–10). As a child of God, you have the assurance that your heavenly Father, out of his grace and mercy, is actively involved in your life (see 1 Peter 2:9–10), even in spite of your natural inadequacies (see Ps. 62:9; Isa. 64:6; John 15:4–5). While you are totally inadequate to live God's way in your own strength, God has chosen you to be a testimony of his love to the world.

We have redemption (the restoration and fulfillment of God's purpose) through Christ, and because he died for us, we are new and changed people—the Bible says "a new creature" (1 Cor. 5:17). Because of him and our faith in what he did for us, we are redeemed. However, we have to work on the change process. We cannot go into a marriage with the same thoughts and behaviors we had when we were single. Why? Because we are now married. We have to build our marriage anew, incorporating new family traditions and rules. For example, one spouse may have received many spankings during his or her childhood, but the other did not. How will your family handle discipline? Furthermore, what does the Bible—not the world—say about spankings? (Read Proverbs 23:13–14.)

As I mentioned in chapter 1, all kinds of chaos broke loose in my marriage because I was neglecting God. I wasn't developing my relationship with him because I was too focused on my natural relationship with my husband. I didn't seek answers from God until the trials and tribulations came. Just like older children don't seek answers from you because they think they know it all. That is how most of us are when we get married. God and his Word are nowhere in sight. He is the one who created the marriage covenant, and he knows all—so why wouldn't you ask him on a daily basis how to deal with your spouse? Proverbs 3:5–6 says, "Trust in the LORD with all thine heart, and lean not unto thine own understanding. In all thy ways acknowledge him, and he shall direct thy paths." We need to seek God on a daily basis regarding how we are to accomplish things pertaining to all of our relationships.

Once you are married, you have to balance your time with God between your spouse, your children, your household responsibilities, your career, and a myriad of other things. Because of all the new demands on your life, you have to become very skilled in finding opportunities to spend quality time with God while still meeting the needs of your spouse and family. Most marriages fail because spouses haven't found a way to do that.

It really is not hard to change or to do the things discussed in this book. In 1 Corinthians 11:1, Paul writes that we should follow his example because he imitated Christ. The Bible gives us an example of how we can do the things our Father has written for us to do; that example is Jesus. Jesus had to die so the Comforter, the Holy Spirit, could come and dwell inside every born-again Christian to comfort us, help us, and guide us throughout our lives. It is the Holy Spirit within you that will help you and teach you how to be a great husband or wife suitable to meet the needs of your spouse and able to understand your individual role so that you can live happily and peacefully. The ministry of the Holy Spirit is vital to helping each of you identify your specific roles and is there to comfort you in the difficult and challenging times that you will encounter during the course of your marriage.

When I was desperate and in utter despair regarding my marriage, I had to seek God and his will. I had to lay aside all of my preconceived ideas about how a marriage should work and open myself to hear from God. I had to open my Bible and get instruction from my heavenly Father about his plan and purpose for marriage. He gave me exactly that. By his Spirit, he led me step by step in learning how to stop my marriage from ending in divorce. Just as God did this for me, he will do it for you. God is no respecter of persons, but he is looking for a willing and obedient vessel that he can speak to and work through to do his will. Once you can identify what he is telling you through the Word of God, the grace (or the power of God working on your behalf) and provisions are available for you to carry out his plan for your life.

Identify Biblically

Why should I, as a Christian, identify biblically? The Bible tells us that when you hear the word of truth preached and believe that Jesus Christ shed his blood for you, you are marked (sealed with the Holy Spirit) as belonging to him (see Eph. 1:13). The very first blessing (gift) that we receive when we accept Jesus as our Savior is the Holy Spirit. Once we accept Christ, we should begin the process of converting from our old ways and ideas and becoming new people in Christ, adopting God's identity and plans for our lives. This includes identifying, understanding, and accepting the roles God created and purposed so that our families would glorify him and be a blessing to humanity on earth. Romans 8:19 states, "For [even the whole] creation (all nature) waits expectantly and longs earnestly for God's sons to be made known [waits for the revealing, the disclosing of their sonship]" (AMP). People are waiting to see

God. You are the closest that some may get to experiencing God. Can people see that you are a son or daughter of God? How do you know if you are a son or daughter of God? Romans 8:14 says, "For all who are led by the Spirit of God are sons of God" (AMP).

Those who *identify biblically* are those who will let the Holy Spirit guide them into all truth and help them in every situation of their lives. It is the Holy Spirit within you who will teach you how to have a better marriage. When you can hear from God and obey the leading of the Holy Spirit, you have become a son or daughter of God.

> **Prayer**
>
> *Father, in the name of Jesus, I ask you to change me. Today I make a quality decision to do your will and do it your way. I will take my eyes and thoughts off my spouse and turn myself over to you. Do a work in me that would help me become a better spouse. Father, thank you for your Spirit inside me, who will lead me into all truth. Thank you that my truth added to your truth (the Word of God) will bring freedom and change to my life. Thank you that my steps are ordered by you; therefore, I can be and do all you ask me to. I shall be the woman of God (or man of God) you are calling me to be because I am willing to change. I know that it is possible, because with you all things are possible. I decree and declare that I am a new person in Christ Jesus, and my light and life will shine before all men so that they will see the glory of God! In Jesus's Name, amen.*

For more on this subject, visit www.marriage101.us for the free article "In Sickness and in Health."

ALTRU**I**SM:
Identify Biblically

In every marriage more than a week old, there are grounds for divorce.
The trick is to find, and continue to find, grounds for marriage.

Robert Anderson

The goal of this section is to help you identify with Christ, or *identify biblically*. Did you know that the Bible gives clear instructions regarding the marriage covenant? Did you also know that once you give your life to Christ, you become one with him? The same holds true for marriages: a man and woman give themselves to one another and become one. Therefore, they are known as husband and wife in the marriage covenant. Your new identity is based on whom you are connected with (are in covenant with). When I accepted Christ, I began identifying myself as a person in Christ (a Christian), and when I got married, I took on my new identity as Mrs. Powell. We all have a responsibility to see what the marriage covenant entails and how to bring it into harmony. Living a Christian life and having a marriage that is pleasing to the Father doesn't just happen overnight. They require that both partners in the marriage covenant are willing to put in the necessary work (yes, *work*) to have the satisfying, fulfilling life that the Bible has promised. This section will provide you with the necessary tools to help you identify with Christ and to fulfill your role as a husband or wife. The start to a "happily ever after" marriage is to let go of who you *were* and become who you *are* in Christ by allowing the Holy Spirit to guide and teach you. Anyone who is willing to make the changes that God reveals is a person who has found their new *identity in Christ,* and the result is a happy, fulfilling marriage the way God intended.

Biblical Example: Ruth and Boaz (Ruth 1–4)

Ruth was a Moabite who left her family, land, and gods to marry and follow an Israelite. Ruth was married to Naomi's son Mahlon. When Naomi's husband and sons died, she decided to return to Bethlehem. At this point Ruth was no longer obligated to Naomi, her mother-in-law, because she was childless and a foreigner. Nevertheless, Ruth insisted on going with Naomi, saying, "Urge me not to leave you or to turn back from following you; for where you go I will go, and where you lodge I will lodge. Your people shall be my people and your God my God" (Ruth 1:16 AMP). In those days widows were looked upon poorly. Unless a close relative redeemed her, Ruth would live a poor and miserable life. Naomi returned to Bethlehem, looking for a kinsman-redeemer. A "kinsman-redeemer" is a relative who has the right to protect the interests of another, especially in the case of financial diffi-culties. In Bethlehem the women met Boaz, a relative of Naomi and a man of great wealth. Ruth worked in Boaz's field, and he favored her because of what he heard about her: "You have left your father and mother and the land of your birth and have come to a people unknown to you before" (Ruth 2:11 AMP). Ruth was sent by Naomi to ask Boaz to become her husband (to protect and provide for her—to act as a kinsman-redeemer). He agreed, even though it meant giving up his heritage and allowing their children to belong to the house of Mahlon, her first husband. Boaz's love and compassion for Ruth was a selfless act. He was a man of honor and dignity. Boaz and the entire city admired Ruth "for all the city of my people know that you are a woman of strength" (or a virtuous woman; Ruth 3:11 AMP). In addition, the women of the city acknowledged her faithfulness and the unconditional love of Naomi as being better than having seven sons.

This couple demonstrates Jesus's love for the church. Both had a selfless love for one another and for their families. Boaz understood his role as a kinsman-redeemer and what it entailed (in this case, losing his heritage). Ruth understood her role as an Israelite. Ruth wanted to follow God and to continue in her role as a child of God, even when she didn't have to. We should be able to identify with this story because like Ruth, we were foreigners, not knowing God, and just as Boaz redeemed Ruth, Jesus's death has redeemed us from sin and death. Jesus gave his life as "a ransom for many" (Mark 10:45). Entering into a union with Christ comes not through birth or ancestry but by accepting Christ and exemplifying Christ in character and unconditional love by conforming our lives to the will of God through obedience to his Word. The greatest bond a husband and wife can share is their faith. The greatest gift to the world is to see a couple demonstrate Jesus's love, which is a selfless and unconditional love. Now that is *identifying biblically*!

Scripture Meditation

Meditate on the following Scriptures to help you fully comprehend your new identity in Jesus Christ. They should help you to transform your attitudes and behaviors so that you better reflect the nature of our Savior. Write down anything God reveals to you in the space after each verse.

1 Corinthians 7:32 (Message)

"I want you to live as free of complications as possible. When you're unmarried, you're free to concentrate on simply pleasing the Master."

(Note: This verse is for singles only.)

_____

_____

_____

_____

_____

_____

2 Corinthians 5:17

"Therefore if any man be in Christ, he is a new creature: old things are passed away; behold, all things are become new."

_____

_____

_____

_____

_____

_____

Ephesians 4:22–24 (AMP)

"Strip yourselves of your former nature [put off and discard your old unrenewed self] which characterized your previous manner of life and becomes corrupt through lusts and desires that spring from delusion; And be constantly renewed in the spirit of your mind [having a fresh mental and spiritual attitude], And put on the new nature (the regenerated self) created in God's image, [Godlike] in true righteousness and holiness."

---

2 Peter 1:3–9 (Message)

"Everything that goes into a life of pleasing God has been miraculously given to us by getting to know, personally and intimately, the One who invited us to God. The best invitation we ever received! We were also given absolutely terrific promises to pass on to you—your tickets to participation in the life of God after you turned your back on a world corrupted by lust. So don't lose a minute in building on what you've been given, complementing your basic faith with good character, spiritual understanding, alert discipline, passionate patience, reverent wonder, warm friendliness, and generous love, each dimension fitting into and developing the others. With these qualities active and growing in your lives, no grass will grow under your feet, no day will pass without its reward as you mature in your experience of our Master Jesus. Without these qualities you can't see what's right before you, oblivious that your old sinful life has been wiped off the books."

Ephesians 5:25–33

"Husbands, love your wives, even as Christ also loved the church, and gave himself for it; That he might sanctify and cleanse it with the washing of water by the word, that he might present it to himself a glorious church, not having spot, or wrinkle, or any such thing; but that it should be holy and without blemish. So ought men to love their wives as their own bodies. He that loveth his wife loveth himself. For no man ever yet hated his own flesh; but nourisheth and cherisheth it, even as the Lord the church: For we are members of his body, of his flesh, and of his bones. For this cause shall a man leave his father and mother, and shall be joined unto his wife, and they two shall be one flesh. This is a great mystery: but I speak concerning Christ and the church. Nevertheless let every one of you in particular so love his wife even as himself; and the wife see that she reverence her husband."

_____

_____

_____

_____

_____

_____

Romans 8:14–17 (AMP)

"For all who are led by the Spirit of God are sons of God. For [the Spirit which] you have now received [is] not a spirit of slavery to put you once more in bondage to fear, but you have received the Spirit of adoption [the Spirit producing sonship] in [the bliss of] which we cry, Abba (Father)! Father! The Spirit Himself [thus] testifies together with our own spirit, [assuring us] that we are children of God. And if we are [His] children, then we are [His] heirs also: heirs of God and fellow heirs with Christ [sharing His inheritance with Him]; only we must share His suffering if we are to share His glory."

_____

_____

_____

_____

_____

Self-Examination

1. What three issues are my spouse and I facing right now that show that neither of us is properly functioning in our God-ordained roles?

2. What can we do to resolve these issues (e.g., forgive, repent, submit, or compromise)?

3. What new traditions, values, or rules do we need to incorporate into our relationship?

4. *For women only*: Read Proverbs 31:10–31 and Titus 2:3–5. Identify three goals you are willing to work toward in order to become a virtuous woman. Then start working toward them until you reach your goal. For example, you may need to better control your tongue. Proverbs 31:26 ("She openeth her mouth with wisdom; and in her tongue is the law of kindness") may be a good verse for you to meditate on as you strive to improve in this area.

5. *For men only*: Find one man in the Bible (such as Abraham, David, Paul, or Moses) and identify three godly leadership characteristics he exhibits that you are willing to work toward possessing in order to become a man of valor. Look for leadership characteristics in his story and then start developing them until you reach your goal. All of these biblical characters made mistakes, but what did God say about them and which would you like to be known for? (For example, David was a man after God's own heart. Moses knew God face to face. Enoch walked with God.)

Developing Character

For men only: Ask yourself, "Do I understand my role as a husband as shown in God's Word?" If you are unaware of your role as a husband, spend some time reading and meditating on Ephesians 5:21–33 in addition to the other Scriptures mentioned in this chapter. In order to ensure that you understand your role, write a brief description based on the Scriptures just reviewed and found throughout the book. Make this your daily confession.

For women only: Ask yourself, "Do I understand my role as a wife as shown in God's Word?" If you are unaware of your role as a wife, spend some time reading and meditating on 1 Peter 3:1–9 in addition to the other Scriptures mentioned in this chapter. In order to ensure that you understand your role, write a brief description based on the Scriptures just reviewed and found throughout the book. Make this your daily confession.

Affirmation

Lord, I am what your Word says I am. I can do what your Word says I can do. For I am your workmanship, created in Christ Jesus for good works, which you have planned beforehand for me that I should walk in, living the good life that you have prearranged and made ready for us to live.

Reflections

_____

_____

_____

_____

_____

_____

_____

_____

_____

_____

_____

_____

_____

_____

_____

_____

3

The Evil One

An Enemy Who Seeks to Devour

Be sober, be vigilant; because your adversary the devil, as a roaring lion, walketh about, seeking whom he may devour.

1 Peter 5:8

The devil and evil spirits are real. I really don't like talking about the enemy, but I have to because the Bible tells us that we do have an adversary. We need to know how to defeat the enemy so we can have victory in every area of our lives, especially in our marriages. The enemy wants you to do everything that is contrary to the Word of God, the things of God, and the people of God. The enemy's influence will cause you to become offended when your mate does something you don't like. His influence can cause you to leave the church and argue with your spouse all the way home. And he can definitely stop your spiritual growth because you can make a decision to do what God has told you one minute, then make excuses as to why you can't do it the next. Even Jesus, when he spent forty days in the wilderness, was tempted by the devil. However, Jesus defeated Satan by quoting what is written by God—the Bible. And just as the evil fairy couldn't kill or destroy Sleeping Beauty, Satan cannot destroy you either.

That Sneaky Devil

This chapter exposes the true enemy who is seeking to destroy your marriage: the devil, not your spouse (see 1 Peter 5:8). The Bible teaches us that the enemy comes to kill, steal, and destroy. He is subtle and sly, waiting for an opportunity to devour God's plan for marriages. By knowing God's plan and purpose for marriage, we can know that we have the victory over the enemy in every battle!

Genesis 2:21–25 tells the story of the first marriage, that of Adam and Eve. Genesis 3 shows that the devil was right there, tempting Eve from the start. Verse 1 says, "Now the serpent was more subtle than any beast." Webster's dictionary defines *subtle* as "so slight as to be difficult to detect or analyze (elusive); skillful or ingenious (clever); marked by craft or slyness (devious); and/or operating in a hidden and usually injurious way (insidious)." That is how the devil works. Satan tempted Adam and Eve by saying, "For God knows that when you eat of it [fruit from the forbidden tree] your eyes will be opened, and you will be like God, knowing good and evil" (Gen. 3:5 NIV). Guess what? Adam and Eve were already like God because God had made them in his own image and likeness. The devil is subtle in that he tricks us into believing something just a little different from what is already true.

He will trick you into believing that your spouse is against you when he or she is not. For example, before you go to bed, your husband asks you to wake him up at 6:30 a.m. because he must attend a very important meeting at 8:00 a.m. You get up at about 6:00 a.m. and start your day. At 7:00 a.m. your husband comes to you angry because you didn't wake him up when you were supposed to. If he took a moment to think about the situation, he would know that you would never do anything intentionally to hurt him. If you tell him that it completely slipped your mind or that you forgot, he should accept it and let it go. Just know that the enemy is the one who will cause him to blow it way out of proportion. Therefore, knowing this, you should not respond with anger.

Your spouse is not your enemy. The devil is, and he will use any situation he can to start an argument and cause strife in your relationship. Division is Satan's purpose because he wants to rule your household. The devil makes you think that your spouse is against you and doesn't want good things for you, but in reality, you would never have married a person who didn't want to do you good all the days of your life.

Know your authority in Christ. If you are a parent, would you let your kids run over you or tell you what to do? No! Then why, as a child of God who has authority over the devil, would you let the devil run your household? Slap him with the Word of God, rebuke him in Jesus's name, and send him packing. I do it daily so that I don't let him rule even for one day. Luke 4:13 says, "And when the devil had ended all the temptation, he departed from [Jesus] for a season." The Word never says that the devil won't come back to tempt you. Therefore, I continue to slap him with my restraining order (the Word of God) so that he and his demons must stay away from me, my family, and my property.

Jesus was tempted by the devil before he began his ministry. In fact, the devil used the Word of God to tempt Jesus (see Matt. 4:1–11). This tells us that we must know the Word. Doesn't it seem as though before you got married, everything was great? I am sure you will admit that your spouse had imperfections, but you loved that person anyway. However, once you got married, the honeymoon quickly ended and the reality of marriage began. Well, it is good to see that the devil is consistent! He shows up when God's plan is about to be made manifest. After Jesus was baptized, the devil came immediately to tempt him (see Luke 4:2). The difference between Christ and us is that he knew the Word of God and was able to rebuke Satan because of his authority. But guess what? He has given us the same authority.

If you submit your life to God and resist and bind the works of the devil, Satan will flee from you (see James 4:7). Know that Satan is after your marriage. As a married couple, you should be magnifying the love of God so people can see God through the witness of your loving union. Please note that not all witnessing is talking. It is also how you live. It is what you do daily without even thinking about it. (We will discuss witnessing more in chapter 8.)

The church is under attack because most of us who go to church and hear the Word are not grounded in the Word. Therefore, persecution comes after we hear the Word, to take away what we just accepted in our hearts to be true (Mark 4:17). The devil comes immediately to take the Word. His purpose is to kill, steal, and destroy (see John 10:10). That includes destroying you, your marriage, and anything that has to do with God. For example, you and your husband attended a marriage conference and as soon as you left, you immediately started arguing.

In many cases, the devil doesn't mess with couples before they get married because they are already sinning—perhaps living with one another, having premarital sex, and so on. Maybe that was or was not the case for you. However, now that you are married, which is a covenant of God, Satan may be using sex to rob your relationship of intimacy and love—perhaps causing you to think of it as a chore or to have no desire for sexual relations. Satan will use anything he can to try to destroy your marriage covenant.

Trials and Tribulations

Every time there is a wedding, it seems as if the devil is plotting, even from that moment, to destroy what God has put together. Most couples are blindsided because they have a fairy-tale wedding, but they also have the naive idea that once the wedding is over they will live happily ever after, with no problems and no work to do. From that point on, the enemy's method is the same. He'll start attacking your mind with impure thoughts or misguided direction, just as he did with Eve. He will attempt to bombard you with thoughts of adultery or jealousy and even try to convince you that you married the wrong person or that your spouse doesn't love you. Once you start to meditate on those thoughts, the truth becomes distorted, and you will start to believe the lies. You will start to make excuses as to why it is okay to sin or to try something that you know is wrong. You may even make excuses for divorce.

temptation: meditating and/or flirting with a thought that is opposite of doing what is right

The Bible instructs us that before those evil thoughts become a reality, we are to cast down every evil thought that tries to exalt itself over the knowledge of God (see 2 Cor. 10:5). This simply means that the evil thoughts will come, but it is our responsibility to counterattack them with God's Word and prayer. All marriages will have trials and tribulations, but God's Word gives us comfort, telling us that blessed is the man or woman who is patient under trial and stands up under temptation (see James 1:12). It is important to know that tests and temptations will come, but they are not from God. God is not the tempter. Since our marriages were created to reflect Christ's love for the church, the devil will do whatever he has to do in order to destroy and kill your marriage. The enemy's "MO" (method of operation) is to have you do or say anything he can that's contrary to the Word of God. Therefore, as Ephesians 6 describes, we must always be girded with the helmet of salvation, the breastplate of righteousness, the sword of truth, and the rest of our spiritual armor to fight the good fight of faith. The Bible instructs us that we are in a war not against flesh and blood but against spiritual principalities in high places (see Eph. 6:12). If we heed our heavenly Father's instructions, we will always win the battle. James tells us:

> Blessed (happy, to be envied) is the man who is patient under trial and stands up under temptation, for when he has stood the test and been approved, he will receive [the victor's] crown of life which God has promised to those who love Him. Let no one say when he is tempted, I am tempted from God; for God is incapable of being tempted by [what is] evil and He Himself tempts no one.
>
> James 1:12–13 AMP

In this passage God is saying that you will be tried and tested and that the devil will tempt you, but this tempting is not of God. What is of God is that you go through and pass the test so that your Father can give you all that he promises. God is a giving God; he only wants to give you his best.

The book of 1 Peter says:

> Be well balanced (temperate, sober of mind), be vigilant and cautious at all times; for that enemy of yours, the devil, roams around like a lion roaring [in fierce hunger], seeking someone to seize upon and devour. Withstand him; be firm in faith [against his onset—rooted, established, strong, immovable, and determined], knowing that the same (identical) sufferings are appointed to your brotherhood (the whole body of Christians) throughout the world. And after you have suffered a little while, the God of all grace [Who imparts all blessing and favor], Who has called you to His [own] eternal glory in Christ Jesus, will Himself complete and make you what you ought to be, establish and ground you securely, and strengthen, and settle you.
>
> 1 Peter 5:8–10 AMP

That passage is so powerful. First of all, note that the enemy is the devil, not your spouse. Second, God is saying that you are not the only one going through hard times in your marriage. So many Christian homes are being ruined because they don't know how to stay rooted, strong, and immovable when they are going through difficulty. This passage also blessed me because God says that after a little while, he will take over and complete you and strengthen you—not your spouse. He is talking to the one who reads it.

When Lewis and I were separated, I asked God for answers, and he gave them. He told me that I needed to change and that I needed to do this, that, and the other. When I asked about Lewis, God told me not to worry about him; that was God's job. As you can see, I had to start the process, but God would finish it. God is now working on Lewis. God is the only one who can change a person to be who he has called them to be.

When trials and tribulations come, just remember that it is only a test. It is not a time to run scared and be defeated; instead, look at the situation as an opportunity for growth and maturity in faith. Paul reminds us of this in his letter to the Romans:

Therefore being justified by faith, we have peace with God through our Lord Jesus Christ: by whom also we have access by faith into this grace in which we stand, and rejoice in hope of the glory of God. And not only so, but we glory in tribulations also, knowing that tribulation worketh patience; and patience, experience; and experience, hope; and hope maketh not ashamed, because the love of God is shed abroad in our hearts by the Holy Ghost which is given unto us.

Romans 5:1–5

Verse 5 in the Amplified version says that "such hope never disappoints or deludes or shames us, for God's love has been poured out in our hearts through the Holy Spirit Who has been given to us." How can it be that when we, who are Christians, are going through times of trial, we feel no love for our spouses? You may think, "I love him, but I don't like him," "She gets on my nerves," or "I don't like the things he does." As Christians, we have the Holy Spirit inside of us leading and guiding us through any challenges we may be facing. The Holy Spirit produces only the fruits of love, joy, peace, patience, kindness, goodness, faithfulness, meekness, and self-control (see Gal. 5:22–23). At some point I realized that I didn't have to work on producing those fruits because they were already in me. So when you're facing challenges in your marriage, go inside yourself and ask God for help, because greater is he that lives on the inside of you than he that is in the world (see 1 John 4:4).

The Big Fight

As I was crying out to the Lord, asking him what had happened in my marriage, God said, "Why do you call me, 'Lord, Lord,' and do not do the things I say?" (see Luke 6:46 NIV). God said that I was denying him because I denied his Word. I attend a Bible-teaching church regularly, I read the Word of God on my own time, I watch Christian television, and I give tithes and offerings. So why was I calling on him when I already knew the right things to do? I knew the answers to my problems were in his Word.

God said that in most areas of my life I was obeying the Word, but I wasn't killing my flesh. And because I was growing spiritually, my flesh and spirit were at odds with one another. I was walking in the Spirit one minute and walking in the flesh the next. This really meant that I was walking with God but still being influenced by the enemy. The devil was the ruler over my marriage because I was still in the flesh when it came to dealing with my husband and our marital issues.

Whenever you are being delivered, being set free, and moving toward the things of God, your flesh is going to wrestle with your spirit. "For our struggle is not against flesh and blood, but against the rulers, against the authorities, against the powers of this dark world and against the spiritual forces of evil in the heavenly realms" (Eph. 6:12 NIV)— that is, we are fighting Satan himself. When we are arguing with our spouses, we know that Satan is behind the confusion, not our spouses. That is why there was warfare in my mind; the Holy Spirit was telling me to do the things of God, but the devil was trying to get me to do things his way. I was trying to make my marriage work based on how the world said it should work, and as my example I was looking at those marriages that have influenced my life (divorced couples, TV, movies, novels, and so on). None of them were a biblical influence.

If we don't do the things God tells us in his Word, Satan has just deceived us, and we have given him control over our marriages. But know that once we start to grow up spiritually, Satan will step up to the plate to stop our growth. The good news is that God only allows the devil to go so far. That's how we know we have the victory—because our Father controls and puts limits on what the devil can do (see Job 1:6–12). We cannot blame God for the struggles we go through. Instead, we need to look at the sin in our lives (acts of disobedience to God's Word) that may have opened the door for Satan to gain entry. Ask God to show you the areas in your life where you have allowed the enemy to deceive you and gain control in your marriage. Repent and ask God to put you on the right track in your marriage. Although God will finish the work, you must start the process: repent and start over at that point of repentance.

In my life, the devil's focus was on how he could separate me not only from my husband but also from the will of God for our lives. God gives us choices—life or death—but he urges us to choose life (see Deut. 30:19). With God there is life, and with the devil there is death. Since God through Jesus Christ has recovered all that the devil stole through Adam and Eve, Satan's purpose is to get as many Christians back under his rule as he can. He doesn't need sinners—those who don't know Christ—because he already has them. So when those thoughts come into your mind like, *It doesn't take all that to be a Christian. It's too hard to be a Christian. I will never be perfect. I am doing pretty good with my life the way it is*, then *you have just been deceived by the enemy.* I used to fall prey to those same thoughts. Now if the enemy tries to tempt me in my thoughts, I immediately pray, find a Scripture that deals with that thought, and ask God to help me concerning that situation.

Satan's Bait

The devil will put ideas in your head—thoughts of adultery or jealous suspicion about someone who works with your mate. Cast out that evil spirit! Don't own the thought or let it stay in your mind. Again, cast down that imagination. For example, if the devil says, "Your husband doesn't love you," turn that thought around and say, "My husband loves me as Christ loves the church" (see Eph. 5:25). Or if the devil says, "You can't get out of the adulterous affair," then say, "I can do all things through Christ who strengthens me" (Phil. 4:13 NKJV). Or if the enemy whispers, "Your husband will never change," then reply, "With man this is impossible, but with God all things are possible" (Matt. 19:26 NIV). In order to defeat the devil, you *must* speak the Word of God. It is like stabbing him with a sword, which is a nickname for the Bible.

Here are some other kinds of bait the devil uses to keep you in the flesh:

1. Lies you tell
2. Mean-spirited words you speak
3. Erroneous and exaggerated thoughts you think (e.g., "All my husband thinks about is sex")
4. Believing the lies he tells you, which are either opposite of the Word of God or twisted (e.g., when the devil was in the garden with Eve, he told her, "You shall not surely die," yet God had told Adam they would surely die)

Here are some things you should do when you sense the devil attacking you:

1. Avoid sinning with your tongue (see Ps. 39:1)
2. Pray and ask God what you should do (see Prov. 3:5–6)
3. Fast (see Matt. 6:16–18)
4. Trust God during this time (see Ps. 37:5)

5. Meditate on God's Word (see Josh. 1:8)
6. Listen to God's voice and do what he tells you to do (see Luke 6:47–48)

Therefore, when you seem to be under an attack, refer to the list above to have victory in your situation.

Defeating the Enemy with God's Word

You can defeat the enemy several ways. However, I will only discuss the way Jesus did it. Jesus communicated with the enemy by quoting the written Word of God. Matthew 4 tells us:

> Then Jesus was led by the Spirit into the desert to be tempted by the devil. After fasting forty days and forty nights, he was hungry. The tempter came to him and said, "If you are the Son of God, tell these stones to become bread." Jesus answered, "It is written: 'Man does not live on bread alone, but on every word that comes from the mouth of God.'" Then the devil took him to the holy city and had him stand on the highest point of the temple. "If you are the Son of God," he said, "throw yourself down. For it is written: '"He will command his angels concerning you, and they will lift you up in their hands, so that you will not strike your foot against a stone.'" Jesus answered him, "It is also written: 'Do not put the Lord your God to the test.'" Again, the devil took him to a very high mountain and showed him all the kingdoms of the world and their splendor. "All this I will give you," he said, "if you will bow down and worship me." Jesus said to him, "Away from me, Satan! For it is written: 'Worship the Lord your God, and serve him only.'" Then the devil left him, and angels came and attended him.
>
> Matthew 4:1–11 NIV

Not only is it important for you to speak God's Word, but it is also just as important that you talk to your spouse with love and respect. Again, they are not your enemy, so your words and the manner in which you communicate with them are critical to having harmonious relationships. As you learn to speak the truth in love, you must also determine when to speak and how to speak. According to Proverbs 18:21, life and death are in the power of the tongue. Therefore, it is important that you pay close attention to the words that are coming from your mouth. This is especially true when communicating with your spouse. For example, I have a loud voice and speak aggressively, so I am constantly monitoring the tone of my voice when talking to my husband so that I won't offend him or seem disrespectful.

Biblical communication is defined as speaking the truth in love (see Eph. 4:15).

> **communication:** expressing and exchanging ideas effectively through speech, writing, or physical contact. Effective communication also includes choosing the best time to talk with your mate.

Sometimes you may find it hard to talk with your mate for fear of an argument erupting or being criticized for your feelings. However, it is impossible to have a great marriage without effective communication and openness. As you may have realized by now, your spouse is not a mind reader. When a problem or circumstance arises, you must tell your mate how you feel and then discuss how you both can meet the needs of one another in that particular situation. Developing a healthy line of communication will help facilitate the avenue for each of you to discuss your feelings and concerns without feeling ashamed or condemned. For example, many couples feel uncomfortable talking about sex. This was a topic that my husband and I had to sit down and discuss. This was not an easy issue to talk about because I was satisfied, but he was not. We had to work through an issue that required us to communicate our feelings without becoming offended, and it definitely required both of us to compromise in order to meet each other's needs. Although this was an uncomfortable topic, we came into agreement and are now on our way to a more satisfying and intimate relationship.

At all times our words should edify, exhort, and bring comfort to the one to whom we are speaking. Even if your husband or wife has done something to hurt or offend you, that does not give you a license to retaliate. You have to learn the art form of knowing what to say, how to say it, and when to say it. Before you speak, ask yourself: Will my words be hurtful? Should I respond right now? Is what I am about to say necessary? I know for me, someone may say something over and over that I disagree with or that I do not like. I may not confront them because I don't want to argue, but in my mind I am thinking, "If they say such-and-such one more time, I am going to go off!" Of course, they inevitably do, so I go off. It is wrong to let something build up until it erupts like a volcano and you hurt someone by what you say, especially when you could have discussed it beforehand without all the frustration and anger.

Some keys to communicating with your spouse are:

- listening attentively while your spouse is speaking, rather than concentrating on what you are going to say in response;
- learning to want the same things (for example, that you both want to live debt-free or to have a happy, fulfilling marriage);
- making direct eye contact;
- thinking before you speak, thereby ensuring that you speak your words with love;
- praying together;
- dreaming together and writing the vision you share for your life;
- knowing your spouse and why they do what they do (for example, is it based on her upbringing? his military background? being from a single-parent home?);

- knowing what your spouse expects from you (such as dinner every night or a phone call to let them know you are okay);
- understanding what your mate is trying to say;
- remembering that your spouse is not a mind reader;
- forgiving one another;
- complimenting and saying "I love you" and "I appreciate you" to your spouse often;
- knowing the best time to talk with your mate;
- conducting family meetings regularly.

Sometimes the best way to communicate with your spouse is to just shut your mouth if an argument has erupted, especially when they are acting foolish. A man or woman of few words and a settled mind is wise. Proverbs 17:28 implies that even a fool is thought to be wise when he is silent. Therefore, it pays for him to keep his mouth shut and control the tongue. I encourage you to think before speaking and know when silence is best. Of course, I am not telling you to go for days without speaking to your spouse. But give yourself or them enough time to cool down. Proverbs 14:1 talks about how a wise woman builds her house, but a foolish woman pulls it down with her hands. This Scripture, of course, is not speaking of a woman physically building and tearing down a house. It represents how she builds her home by making wise choices in her relationships with her husband and children. Wise men and women will continually build upon their relationship and not allow it to become stagnant or tear it down.

Proverbs 12:14 states, "A man will be satisfied with good by the fruit of his words" (NASB). Some time ago my husband clearly saw for himself the fruit of his words. Every time someone would ask him about us, he would tell them, "It is messed up!" or "We are not getting along," or "Our sex life is terrible." He then recognized that people developed a negative perception of our marriage based on what he said. The next time those same people would see him, they would talk negatively about me or speak of us getting a divorce. He realized he had to change their image, so he started to speak (confess) what was good in our marriage.

> **confession:** acknowledgment or profession of belief, faith, or sins

Confessing the good allowed him to change his view of me because he stopped focusing on the negative. We must be careful not to focus too much on what is wrong in our marriages. The shield of faith (see Eph. 6:16) allows us to look into the invisible world of a good marriage rather than being blinded by the temporary situation of a bad marriage. Therefore, our confession is not hypocritical—it's our faith speaking.

When arguments arise, the best way to resolve them is to immediately find solutions. Many couples may drag an argument on and on, which may lead to days of not communicating. This gives the enemy an opening to kill, steal, or destroy your relationship. For example, say you have told your mate, in so many words, that you don't like a particular thing they do; yet they continue to do it. In your mind you have already established that if they do it again, you are not going to say anything. Therefore, out of anger, you don't speak for days. That is a *no-no*. Instead, you should find the best time to sit down and communicate with your spouse about the situation and find ways to resolve it. You cannot say, "You need to change." You both need to come to an agreement on how the argument can be resolved and what each person can do to help the situation.

> **agreement:** harmony of opinion; the act of at least two people uniting on a particular issue or concern

Every time you come into agreement about how to deal with a situation, you are establishing a covenant. I describe the covenants we have as "mini-contracts." Lewis and I have established several that we have agreed to honor until death or until we agree to modify the terms. For example, our agreement regarding our sex life is a covenant. So is our agreement regarding the days I cook and don't cook, and so on. What are some of your covenants that you and your spouse have agreed to?

Talk Biblically

Why is it so important that we talk (communicate) biblically? When we accepted Jesus Christ into our lives, we became soldiers for him. It is just like being in the military: if you signed up to become a soldier, you must surrender your mind, will, and emotions to conform to the military's standards. As Scripture says, "No soldier when in service gets entangled in the enterprises of [civilian] life; his aim is to satisfy and please the one who enlisted him" (2 Tim. 2:4 AMP). A soldier's heart is to serve his country and to serve his branch of the military honorably. That is what our aim should be when we become enlisted in the army of the Lord. Our desire should be to honor and serve God by being diligent and obedient to do the things he has instructed us to do in his Word. In this case that includes how we communicate with our spouses and others. And just like the military takes care of all of its soldiers' needs, God also provides his children—you—with everything you need when you are enlisted under his care.

Ephesians 6:11 puts it this way: "Put on God's whole armor [the armor of a heavy-armed soldier which God supplies], that you may be able successfully to stand up against [all] the strategies and the deceits of the devil" (AMP). In order to defeat the enemy, we must use God's armor, which is listed in Ephesians 6:14–18. Be sure to use the helmet of salvation and the sword of the Spirit, which is the Word of God. They will help to protect your thoughts and actions. For example, the enemy will test you in three ways: (1) the lust of the flesh; (2) the lust of the eyes; and (3) the pride of life (see 1 John 2:16). In order to defeat the enemy, as Jesus did, you must speak the Word. For example, say you are a married man and you meet a beautiful woman who just started working in your office. She tells you that you are handsome and charming. You are then consumed with thoughts about asking her to lunch: "It's only lunch. She's beautiful. Your wife hasn't told you lately that you were handsome." To stop those thoughts, you must start quoting Scripture: "I love my wife as Christ loves the church. I shall not commit adultery. The enemy comes to kill, steal, and destroy my marriage. I love my wife and children." Then run (excuse yourself immediately) from that situation. Protect yourself by establishing appropriate boundaries with that person, and any others who tempt you, by never putting yourself in a position where you are alone with them.

Prayer

Father, I pray that you will reveal to me and [name your spouse] ways in which we can communicate to one another more effectively. Show me where I fall short as a man or woman of God. Help me to bridle my tongue. Teach me how to speak the truth in love and to know what and when to speak so that I can edify, exhort, and bring comfort to my man or woman of God. As Psalm 19 says, let the words of my mouth and the meditation of my heart be acceptable in your sight, O Lord, my Strength and my Redeemer. I thank you that you have given me authority to bind all things that work against me and to release your power through your Word. I thank you that your Word is truth and I don't have to live a lie and that my marriage can and will be all that you have designed it to be. I cast out all things (bitterness, hatred, anger, criticisms) that may irritate my spouse and cause me to stir up strife. Help me to defeat the enemy when he tries to attack my marriage and my family. Thank you, Lord. Amen.

For more on this subject, visit www.marriage101.us for a free copy of the article "Fifteen Ways to Communicate Effectively."

alTRUISM:
Talk Biblically

> The curse which lies upon marriage is that too often the individuals are joined in their weakness rather than in their strength—each asking from the other instead of finding pleasure in giving.
>
> Simone de Beauvoir

The goal of this section is to help you better communicate by learning how to *talk biblically*—using the Bible as a weapon to defeat the enemy. Are you doubting what God has said concerning your marriage? How many times have you spoken death into your marriage by saying, "I want a divorce!" "I don't love you anymore!" or "I hate you!" The purpose of this chapter is to help you and your spouse learn to speak the same things in faith and to work on ways to improve your communication. It will allow you to take inventory of the words that you are speaking to see whether they are destroying your marriage or building it up. Jesus defeated the enemy with the Word of God, and you can too, because the Word is your defense and shield. A person who knows how to use the weapons God gave us will always be victorious. Therefore, speak the Word only—*talk biblically*.

Biblical Example: Job and His Wife (The Book of Job)

The book of Job is about a man who suffered the loss of his children, servants, livestock, herdsmen, home, and health—yet he continued to trust and love the God he served. Job 2:3 says, "And the Lord said to Satan, Have you considered My servant Job, that there is none like him on the earth, a blameless and upright man, one who [reverently] fears God and abstains from and shuns all evil [because it is wrong]? And still he holds fast his integrity"—[Note: The New International Reader's Version Bible says, "He still continues to be faithful"]—"although you moved Me against him to destroy him without cause" (AMP). Yes, bad things do happen to good people. And good things happen to bad people. Since we live in an evil world, some trials and situations just can't be avoided. For example, terrorist attacks, drunk drivers, the choices of evil people, tsunamis, etc. When we face these things we shouldn't question God as to *why* these things happen but should simply trust him and allow him to do a work in us and through us when they do. God does not tempt us with evil. Although he allows bad things to happen, he does it to humble us and prove us faithful so he can bless us in the end (see Deut. 8:16). God ultimately wants to purify us. He wants us to depend on him, to help others, and to confess and repent of sin in our lives.

Only God knows why things happen, and we must trust our sovereign God. We must not do what Job's wife did. Job 2:9 says, "His wife said to him, 'Are you still continuing to be faithful to the Lord? Speak evil things against him and die!'" (NIrV). However, consider Job's rebuttal: "'You talk like a foolish woman. Should we accept only good things from the hand of God and never anything bad?' So in all this, Job said nothing wrong" (v. 10 NLT).

I love this couple because they remind me of most married couples. Job was the only person standing on the Word of God; his wife, even though she was a woman of faith, was talking as a heathen (someone who does not know God). Let me say to those in similar situations: there is hope for those who want their relationships to work, even if the other person is acting foolishly and talking like a heathen. If your marriage is going through a difficult time, stand on God's Word and hear from him concerning what you should do in your situation.

Never reject God or his commandments when you are being tested. God doesn't owe us anything. Therefore, we can only trust him, even when we don't understand why we are going through the struggles in our lives. Our love for God and for one another will be tested. Will you curse God or will you continue to trust him? Hold on to your faith through trials and tribulations and know that God will reward your faithfulness. In the end, God gave Job twice as much as he had before he went through his trial.

Scripture Meditation

Meditate on the following Scriptures to determine whether or not you *talk biblically*. These Scriptures will help you change the way you speak to your spouse so that you are speaking to him or her in love, which is a start to building a healthy, stronger marriage. Write down anything God reveals to you in the space after each verse.

Psalm 119:172

"My tongue shall speak of thy word: for all thy commandments are righteousness."

_____

_____

_____

Matthew 12:34–37

"O generation of vipers, how can ye, being evil, speak good things? for out of the abundance of the heart the mouth speaketh. A good man out of the good treasure of the heart bringeth forth good things: and an evil man out of the evil treasure bringeth forth evil things. But

I say unto you, That every idle word that men shall speak, they shall give account thereof in the day of judgment. For by thy words thou shalt be justified, and by thy words thou shalt be condemned."

_____

_____

_____

_____

_____

Amos 3:3

"Can two walk together, except they be agreed?"

_____

_____

_____

_____

_____

1 Peter 3:8–12 (Message)

"Summing up: Be agreeable, be sympathetic, be loving, be compassionate, be humble. That goes for all of you, no exceptions. No retaliation. No sharp-tongued sarcasm. Instead, bless—that's your job, to bless. You'll be a blessing and also get a blessing.

Whoever wants to embrace life
 and see the day fill up with good,
Here's what you do:
 Say nothing evil or hurtful;
Snub evil and cultivate good;
 run after peace for all you're worth.

God looks on all this with approval,
    listening and responding well to what he's asked;
But he turns his back
    on those who do evil things."

_____

_____

_____

_____

Ephesians 6:13–18 (AMP)

"Therefore put on God's complete armor, that you may be able to resist and stand your ground on the evil day [of danger], and having done all [the crisis demands], to stand [firmly in your place]. Stand therefore [hold your ground], having tightened the belt of truth around your loins and having put on the breastplate of integrity and of moral rectitude and right standing with God, and having shod your feet in preparation [to face the enemy with the firm-footed stability, the promptness, and the readiness produced by the good news] of the Gospel of peace. Lift up over all the [covering] shield of saving faith, upon which you can quench all the flaming missiles of the wicked [one]. And take the helmet of salvation and the sword that the Spirit wields, which is the Word of God. Pray at all times (on every occasion, in every season) in the Spirit, with all [manner of] prayer and entreaty. To that end keep alert and watch with strong purpose and perseverance, interceding in behalf of all the saints (God's consecrated people)."

_____

_____

_____

_____

Self-Examination

1. Do I communicate with my spouse effectively? If not, what can I do to improve our communication? If yes, how can I improve it to make it better than what it is?

2. Can I be transparent before my mate? If not, why not? What are some ways I can begin to open up without fear?

3. What are some topics that we need to discuss? Pray about them and schedule a family meeting to discuss them.

4. In what ways is the enemy trying to tempt me? Write down some Scriptures you can use to defeat the attacks.

5. Do we have a vision for our family? If not, schedule a family meeting to develop one and write it down. Start with what you want for your family (such as the number of children, health and financial goals, whether to start a business, a peaceful home, and so on). Then set a one-year goal for each topic. For example, you may work toward your financial goals by paying off three credit cards by the end of the year, saving $250 a month, or starting a stock portfolio. Of course, this may take several monthly meetings, but start the process. Every month, check on your progress.

Developing Character

For an entire week, listen to yourself. Do you speak what is good and pleasing to your spouse and God? Or do you speak what is wrong and displeasing? Did you curse this week? Did you shut up when the Holy Spirit told you to? Did you speak words that do not line up with Scripture (such as telling your spouse that you hate them, even though God's Word says for us to love one another)? At the end of the week, determine whether your words are building up or destroying your house. Write down those things that you too often speak that may destroy your marriage. Then find Scriptures that will help you bring life back into your marriage. Start speaking life into your situation.

Affirmation

Every time I open my mouth, the wisdom of God comes out and the law of kindness is on my tongue.

Reflections

_____

_____

_____

_____

_____

_____

_____

4

Honor the King

Submit One to Another

Submit to one another out of reverence for Christ.

Eph. 5:21 NIV

We all have someone in a position of higher authority to whom we must answer. As an employee, you submit to your supervisor. In a marriage, wives are to submit to their own husbands, and husbands are to submit to Christ. Therefore, husbands are to honor their head (the King of Kings) by loving their wives unconditionally in spite of what their wives may or may not be doing—just as Jesus did for us. Wives are to honor their husbands (the king of their home) through submission and respect, just as they would submit to their King—Christ. We even see authority in the story of Sleeping Beauty: the townspeople submitted to the king's authority to get rid of all of their spinning wheels. Submission to one another is what we do unto God and out of reverence for God.

Submission

Submission is a new way of thinking for men and women. Both men and women are to submit to one another. But first we must stop thinking that the word *submit* means to be ruled and dominated. The *Student Bible Dictionary* definition of *submission* and *submit* is this: "Yield. Christian submission is to voluntarily yield in love and consider another's needs more important than one's own." It is not an act; it is an attitude of the heart.

> **submit:** to yield oneself to the will or authority of another; to assist or help carry out the vision of another

Both men and women are to submit themselves one to another in the fear of God. Your position as a married person should always be looking toward your spouse and asking them, "What can I do for you?" or "How can I help you today?" I was taught in premarital class to have this attitude (and mean it): *I live to please my man (or woman) of God.* How do we submit to our husband or wife? Philippians 2:3–5 says,

Do nothing from factional motives [through contentiousness, strife, selfishness, or for unworthy ends] or prompted by conceit and empty arrogance. Instead, in the true spirit of humility (lowliness of mind) let each regard the others as better than and superior to himself [thinking more highly of one another than you do of yourselves]. Let each of you esteem and look upon and be concerned for not [merely] his own interests, but also each for the interests of others. Let this same attitude and purpose and [humble] mind be in you which was in Christ Jesus: [Let him be your example in humility].

AMP

humility: considering another person more
important than yourself; freedom from pride and
arrogance

I believe this next verse talks of submission as supporting your
husband's mission: "Wives, be subject (be submissive and adapt
yourselves) to your own husbands as [a service] to the Lord" (Eph.
5:22 AMP). Submission simply means to humble yourself before
God—not before man or woman but before God. Both men and
women have a responsibility to display an attitude of submitting to
one another.

Again, your spouse is not your enemy. Think of submission as
humbling yourself before God, not your mate. God's Word says to
"submit yourselves to every ordinance of man *for the Lord's sake*"
(1 Peter 2:13, emphasis added). Queen Vashti, according to the
book of Esther, decided she did not want to submit to the king when
he requested her presence at his party. Because she was the king's
glory, he wanted to show her off as the beautiful woman she was.
However, she took it upon herself to see his request as an offense.
She was probably thinking, "I am not going out there in front of
all those drunken men." She looked at it as honoring her husband
instead of as honoring God through submission.

Since the marriage relationship is reflective of Jesus's love for
the church, it is imperative that biblical submission and love be
practiced in all aspects of the relationship between a husband and
wife. Biblical submission is an attitude of the heart, which is demonstrated by serving others and regarding others as more important
than yourself. This does not mean that you place yourself under the
control of another but means that you stand directly accountable
to God.

Let's consider a personal example. Suppose that you and your
husband are at a dinner party, and in the middle of the conversation,
he asks you to get him something to drink. Do you think, "Who

does he think I am? He should go get it himself," and actually make him get it? No, this is an opportunity to submit, honor your man of God, and be a witness to others of Christ in you. Humble yourself before God, not your mate. I have finally come to a place where I see being submissive as simply honoring my man of God. (Notice that I didn't say honoring Lewis. Saying "man of God" may help us see them differently than just as mere men.)

When God talks about the man being the head of the woman, he is not talking about ability or worth, competence or value, brilliance or advantage. God is talking about function and order within the partnership. For example, every organization, business, or partnership must have a head in order for it to operate efficiently. Otherwise there will be no guidance, no direction, and no peace. Although God has designated the man to be the head of the home, there may be times when the man should submit to the wife. Remember, the Bible says that you should submit "one to another" (Eph. 5:21). For example, a husband is not strong when it comes to paying bills on time, yet his wife is strong in the area of finances. The best thing for that couple is to use her strength so the household will not be in financial jeopardy. In this particular example, the husband should submit to his wife concerning their finances.

If a wife submits to her husband even though he may be unsaved or a backslider, God can use her submission as a way to win him back for God (see 1 Peter 3:1). Likewise, if a husband who has an unbelieving wife submits to Christ, God can use his submission to help win her to God. To submit to Christ, a man must love his wife unconditionally, just as Christ loves the church. He must love her regardless of what she does or does not do. I believe that one godly person standing on God's Word can turn their marriage around, even if they are married to an unsaved or backslidden spouse, if both want the marriage and at least one person is willing to change. Lewis and I both wanted to stay married, but he didn't know where to begin. I did, so I got the Bible out and started reading about how to be a good wife. Every time God told me through reading the Word to do something, I submitted myself and did it. God's Word works. You just have to work God's Word.

Submission is not an act. It should be the very core of your being. For example, people may say that you are a touchy-feely person, and you say, "That is just who I am." Well, you don't *act* touchy-feely. That is just who you *are*. In the same way, witnessing (showing Jesus's love in you) is not an act; it's what people should see through you. God is trying to tell us to stop acting and actually *become* like Jesus. Just do what the Word says and be more like him. God doesn't have to act nice toward us—he just is. Because we are born again, we have the gift of the Holy Spirit, and he has all we need so that we don't have to act. We just have to be led by him. The Bible tells us that we must submit to someone of higher authority. We are to submit to:

1. God—"Submit yourselves therefore to God" (James 4:7)
2. Husbands and wives—"Submitting yourselves one to another in the fear of God" (Eph. 5:21)
3. Parents—"Children, obey your parents. . . . 'Honor your father and mother'" (Eph. 6:1–2 NIV)
4. Other believers—"All of you be submissive to one another" (1 Peter 5:5 NKJV)
5. Employers—"Servants, be subject to your masters" (1 Peter 2:18)
6. Appointed authority in the church—"You who are younger and of lesser rank, be subject to the elders (the ministers and spiritual guides of the church)—[giving them due respect and yielding to their counsel]. Clothe (apron) yourselves, all of you, with humility [as the garb of a servant, so that its covering cannot possibly be stripped from you, with freedom from pride and arrogance] toward one another" (1 Peter 5:5 AMP)

7. Anyone in authority, including the government—"Submit yourselves to every ordinance of man for the Lord's sake" (1 Peter 2:13)

There is freedom in submission (see Rom. 13:2–5). Jesus submitted to God's will, and as a result, we are free from sin and death. The way we can honor Jesus is to honor others. As Christians we honor individuals not based on any ulterior motives but just because they too have been created in the image and likeness of God and because God loves them.

Honoring God

I have learned that we can honor God, whom we have not seen, by honoring our brethren (especially our spouses), whom we *have* seen.

honor: to show respect and reverence for another

I remember a time when Lewis and I were arguing over me fixing dinner. I told him I would not fix him dinner, and he told me I'd *better*. I was so mad, and we were arguing at the top of our voices, and he walked out. The first thing that came to my mind was, "Wait until he comes home! I will have bread and water waiting for him." The second thought that came was from God.

"Will you honor man or honor me?"

I said, "You, God."

He said, "Then call your man of God, apologize, and ask him what he wants for dinner."

I did just that, and then God said, "What you do unto Lewis you do unto me. You honor me through honoring him."

I remembered the Scripture "Serve wholeheartedly, as if you were serving the Lord, not men" (Eph. 6:7 NIV). I then asked God what had happened. How did Lewis and I even get to that point? Lewis doesn't like leftovers, so he wants a freshly prepared meal every evening. Because of that argument, Lewis and I established a covenant: I would cook every night except Fridays and Saturdays. Moreover, on other nights that I didn't feel like cooking, I would notify him early enough that we could make other plans.

Instead of arguing over and over, we found a solution and worked from there. As Christian couples, we need to get away from "fleshly thinking": "He doesn't tell *me* what to do!" "Who does she think I am?" "I am my own person!" We need to renew our minds. We need to start thinking about how we can honor God through honoring our man or woman of God. This also applies to disagreements with friends, coworkers, parents, and so on. By apologizing and doing what is right in the sight of God, you honor God. It should be easier for us to do when we realize that we aren't bowing to that person but to God. We have to renew our minds and know that if we do what's right, we are not necessarily giving in to that person, but rather, we are honoring God, even if they are wrong. As Christians we are to honor God through serving people, and when we honor him above our own feelings, the love of God in us can love and honor others at all times.

The number one thing, in my opinion, that will stop you from honoring the king or queen in your home is pride. God cannot help those who are having a hard time in their marriage if they are prideful. Why? Because God resists the proud, but he will give grace to the humble (see 1 Peter 5:5).

> **pride:** feeling that you can do things on your own, without the help of God and others, or that the successes of your life are due to your own efforts

Pride is the inner voice that whispers, "I want it done my way!" It tells you that life is about you, which is the very opposite of what

God's Word says. Life is about serving and being a blessing to others. Pride will lead to divorce. When a marriage is suffering from pride, neither party wants to admit they are wrong. Neither wants to apologize to the other or admit they need to change because pride says, "It's his (or her) fault" and "I am okay just the way I am." But God will resist the proud and give grace to the humble (see 1 Peter 5:5). The Lord revealed to me that being humble simply means that Christ in me reigns—or becomes larger—and I become smaller. It is not about me or my feelings but about what he can say or do through me.

Grace

God gives us sufficient grace to do the work of the ministry he has given us. He knew what he was doing when he put you and your spouse together. When your friend says, "If he were my husband, I wouldn't take that," it's because there's no grace for her concerning that man. But there is grace for you when dealing with your husband; that's why he's *your* husband (or why she's your wife, for men). That is also why you can't let people talk you out of what God has in store for you and your spouse. In the book of Esther, King Ahasuerus let his officers (wise men) talk him into divorcing Queen Vashti over her disobedience. They told the king he couldn't let Queen Vashti get away with it, telling him, "What would happen to us if our wives knew what she did? They wouldn't respect us either" (see Esther 1:16–18). In Esther 2:1 we read that when he cooled down, "King Xerxes' anger had cooled and he was having second thoughts about what Vashti had done and what he had ordered against her" (Message). His hasty decision and the counsel of others led him to a place of divorce, where he never wanted to be.

Don't let anyone talk you out of doing God's will. He will give you the grace to hold your marriage together. God gives grace for the husband to be the head and for the wife to be a helpmeet.

> **grace:** God's power and anointing that gives
> you the ability to do what he has called you to do;
> also, the undeserved favor and love of God

Struggles come when you work outside of your role as a husband or a wife, but you will find peace and rest when you work within the grace you've been given. Moreover, when you stop trying to fix the problems in your marriage in your own strength but instead do what is necessary to bring about a change in you and rely on the help (Holy Spirit) that is available, there is a grace that comes to you. When you are weak and can't seem to go on, factor in the grace that God gives you.

As Peter advises:

In the same way you married men should live considerately with [your wives], with an intelligent recognition [of the marriage relation], honoring the woman as [physically] the weaker, but [realizing that you] are joint heirs of the grace (God's unmerited favor) of life, in order that your prayers may not be hindered and cut off. [Otherwise you cannot pray effectively.] Finally, all [of you] should be of one and the same mind (united in spirit), sympathizing [with one another], loving [each other] as brethren [of one household], compassionate and courteous (tenderhearted and humble).

1 Peter 3:7–8 AMP

As Peter stated, we are joint heirs of grace. Men must honor their wives, or, as the Word states, their prayers will be hindered. Being of the same mind is simply submitting yourselves one to another in love for the sake of Christ. Look at Jesus's attitude regarding submission. When the time had come for him to fulfill God's purpose, he prayed, "Father, if thou be willing, remove this cup from me: nevertheless not my will, but thine, be done" (Luke 22:42). Look at his heart. He was saying, "I don't want to, Father, but *nevertheless*, I will because you want me to." That's the kind of attitude we should have.

Mind Your Business

First Corinthians 1:10 states, "Now I beseech you, brethren, by the name of our Lord Jesus Christ, that ye all speak the same thing, and that there be no divisions among you; but that ye be perfectly joined together in the same mind and in the same judgment." One thing that causes division in a marriage is the wife trying to go ahead of her husband. Remember, "If a house be divided against itself, that house cannot stand" (Mark 3:25). Eve let the devil influence her and caused humanity to separate from God. God drove them out of the garden, and mankind's relationship with God changed forever. Division causes a change for the worse. Division is caused by being led by your flesh.

If Eve had listened to God, the devil's influence would not have divided her house. She could have easily purposed in her heart not to eat the fruit because her husband told her not to. That would have been submission. Instead she ate from the tree and gave some to her husband. Then they both sinned and were outside of the will of God. I am not blaming Eve for the fall of man, because ultimately it was Adam's responsibility to say no, since he was the head and God had spoken to him. But women of God, we have to make sure that we are submitted to God and to our husbands to help them do what God has told them to do. By not submitting we open the door, as Eve did, for the enemy to come in and destroy the original plan of God for our lives.

Who (or what) are you going to let divide your household? Your single friends, your unbelieving family members, your own expectations as to what you think something or someone should be? Our mates are who God has made them to be. Who are you to change them or even want them to change? When you start wanting to change someone else, always look inside yourself first. Ask yourself what *you* need to change about your circumstances or situation. God will always tell you about *you*.

Romans 2:1 says, "You, therefore, have no excuse, you who pass judgment on someone else, for at whatever point you judge the other, you are condemning yourself, because you who pass judgment do the same things" (NIV). No matter what we think, we all fall into the trap of judging, and it's deadly to a marriage.

My husband and I were saved before we got married, but Lewis didn't go to church often. I would wake up on Sunday mornings and start nagging, "Are you going to church this morning?"

"No," he would answer.

I would come back with, "Oh, you could go out last night, but you can't get up and go to church. If it were a business meeting, you would get up in a minute!" That's judging.

I used to be a judgmental and nagging wife. I was trying to force Lewis to go to church, and when he didn't, I tried to make him feel guilty. God does not want us to force him on anybody. The best way we can let people know about Jesus is through our godly lifestyle. Lewis didn't start going to church again until he saw a difference in me. When I started submitting to Lewis as the head of our family, he knew there had to be a good God, and he wanted to know him.

God showed me that I needed to mind my own business. Your spouse is not your business; he or she is God's business, and God does not need little gods helping him do his job.

Don't let the devil deceive you into thinking that you are better than your mate, either. You are equals; that is why you can submit to one another. However, women, no matter where you are spiritually, God will not elevate you above your head. As long as I am submissive, we will have no clashes because I know my role as a woman of God. So if you are totally submissive to your man of God, as you increase in the things of God, so will he. My husband has grown spiritually because I have, and he probably doesn't even realize how far he has come. In just one year Lewis started going to church more, he started tithing, praying, and reading the Word more, and he even went to a men's conference. That was big! Whatever the call of God is on your spouse's life, if you submit yourself to that vision or call, then you ultimately are helping your spouse to become all he or she should be.

A Vow unto God

I remember that on the day of my wedding, someone didn't agree with the vows I recited. I guess they thought I was cursing my marriage because I promised to love and stay with Lewis for better or for *worse*, in *sickness* and in health, for richer or *poorer*, until death do us part. When I said it, I meant that no matter what state we were in, we would stay together. However, when the "for worse" came, I kicked him out of the house. A voice from within said, "Will you honor your vow to me?" I have since realized the vow I made on that day was not only to Lewis but to God as well. I also never envisioned having problems in my marriage because we were so in love. Of course we had disagreements prior to marriage, but we overcame those. But for some reason, we couldn't overcome the ones after the wedding. Did I have blinders on? Was I still believing in fairy tales? Or did I just not pay attention during our premarital counseling? Probably all of the above were true, because like most people, I thought our situation would be different after we got married.

I remember asking God why marriage was so tough. I started reading Ecclesiastes 3, which states, "To every thing there is a season, and a time to every purpose under the heaven. . . . A time to break down, and a time to build up; a time to weep, and a time to laugh . . . a time to love, and a time to hate; a time of war, and a time of peace" (vv. 1, 3, 8). To reach your purpose, you have to go through the corresponding season. For me, during our separation we were at "a time to break down," and when we decided we wanted our marriage, it was our "time to build up" (v. 3). All this has caused me to fulfill my purpose, which I am doing right now—encouraging couples to stay married. All marriages have a season of opportunity to experience the times mentioned in Ecclesiastes 3. You made a promise to God and your spouse that during those difficult seasons you would stay. Will you keep the vow you made?

Submit Biblically

I hope that after reading this chapter, you have a better understanding of the word *submit*. But why should you submit biblically? The Greek word for *submit* is *hupotasso*, which means to obey or to be under the authority of someone. Although the Bible tells us to submit to those in authority and higher positions, husbands and wives are to submit one to another (see Eph. 5:21). At the same time, all are to submit to God (see James 4:7). We honor God when we submit to and obey him. To honor God, we must submit to his ways, his statutes, and his commandments. Therefore, when God tells you to do something for your spouse and you do it, even if you don't want to, you have honored God. And when you obey the King by keeping his commandments, the Bible says you can ask anything in his name, and he will give it to you (see John 14:14–15). Just think: your prayers may not be answered because you have not obeyed God concerning your marriage. Honoring one another through submission will demonstrate your love to God. If you are concerned that you are unable to submit to your spouse, God will give you the grace (power) to do what you cannot do on your own. Bottom line, when you honor your spouse, you honor God.

Prayer

Father, I now understand that to honor you, I must honor others, especially my spouse. I submit myself to you and my spouse, knowing that your plan for our marriage is perfect. I will not judge, so that I won't be judged. I will not walk in pride because you resist the proud and give grace to those who humble themselves before you. Teach me how to be humble and walk in the spirit of meekness. Do not let pride hinder me from your grace and perfect plan for me. I receive your grace to be a better wife or husband. Thank you for your Word, which gives me life and freedom. I am free to submit to my spouse and all who are in authority over me, knowing that it honors and pleases you. And Father, I will honor the vow I made to you on my wedding day. Praise you, Jesus! In Jesus's name, amen.

Visit www.marriage101.us for a free copy of the article "Nine Tips to Prevent Divorce."

ALTRUI**S**M:
Submit Biblically

> When you make a sacrifice in marriage, you're sacrificing not to each other but to unity in a relationship.
>
> Joseph Campbell

The goal of this section is to help you *submit biblically*. The topic of submission can raise some tough questions: "How do I submit without feeling like I am giving up who I am?" "How can I honor God's commands when my spouse is not treating me right?" Submitting biblically is saying to God, "Not my will but yours be done." Even Jesus said, "Father, if thou be willing, remove this cup from me: nevertheless not my will, but thine, be done" (Luke 22:42). If we keep the Father in the forefront of our minds, we understand that we obey out of reverence *to God* because of our love *for God*. It takes a strong, mature Christian to do that. Therefore, a person who can surrender their will to others and God is a person who can *submit biblically*.

Biblical Example: King Ahasuerus and Queen Vashti (Esther 1–2:1)

King Ahasuerus was drinking and partying. He summoned his wife, Queen Vashti, to come to his party to parade her beauty in front of all of his companions. She refused to obey. The king was angry and asked his assistants what he should do. Their response was that if he allowed her to get away with her disobedience, all the women would hear about it and would not respect their men. The king listened to them and commanded that she be banished from the kingdom. But after the king cooled off, he regretted his decision. And yet his pride would not allow him to go back to those who counseled him and admit his mistake. As the king, he could have given another command that would allow him to remarry Vashti. Even the Bible says that if you separate or divorce, you should be reconciled to your spouse (see 1 Cor. 7:10–11). However, God had a greater backup plan with Queen Esther.

King Ahasuerus's anger, drunkenness, and wrong counseling were the cause of his divorce, even more than the actions of his wife. We have no idea why Vashti chose not to obey, but we do know that the Bible says the wife should be submissive to her husband in everything (see Eph. 5:24). If she had submitted biblically, more than likely she would not have divorced. And just imagine how she must have felt, going from having it all to being a castaway. Be careful how you respond to offense. It can take you out of the will and blessings of God. In this case, both King Ahasuerus and Queen Vashti suffered due to hasty and unbiblical responses to one another.

Scripture Meditation

Meditate on the following Scriptures, which will help you understand how to submit biblically. Ask yourself, "In what areas of my life do I still refuse to submit to God?" Write down anything God reveals to you about your need to submit biblically in the space after each verse.

Ephesians 5:21–24

"Submitting yourselves one to another in the fear of God. Wives, submit yourselves unto your own husbands, as unto the Lord. For the husband is the head of the wife, even as Christ is the head of the church: and he is the saviour of the body. Therefore as the church is subject unto Christ, so let the wives be to their own husbands in every thing."

_____

_____

_____

_____

1 Peter 3:5–7 (NIV)

"For this is the way the holy women of the past who put their hope in God used to make themselves beautiful. They were submissive to their own husbands, like Sarah, who obeyed Abraham and called him her master. You are her daughters if you do what is right and do not give way to fear. Husbands, in the same way be considerate as you live with your wives, and treat them with respect as the weaker partner and as heirs with you of the gracious gift of life, so that nothing will hinder your prayers."

_____

_____

_____

Colossians 3:23–24

"And whatsoever ye do, do it heartily, as to the Lord, and not unto men; Knowing that of the Lord ye shall receive the reward of the inheritance: for ye serve the Lord Christ."

_____

_____

_____

_____

Philippians 2:3–5 (AMP)

"Do nothing from factional motives [through contentiousness, strife, selfishness, or for unworthy ends] or prompted by conceit and empty arrogance. Instead, in the true spirit of humility (lowliness of mind) let each regard the others as better than and superior to himself [thinking more highly of one another than you do of yourselves]. Let each of you esteem and look upon and be concerned for not [merely] his own interests, but also each for the interests of others. Let this same attitude and purpose and [humble] mind be in you which was in Christ Jesus: [Let Him be your example in humility]."

_____

_____

_____

1 Peter 2:13, 17

"Submit yourselves to every ordinance of man for the Lord's sake: whether it be to the king, as supreme. . . . Honour all men. Love the brotherhood. Fear God. Honour the king."

_____

_____

_____

Self-Examination

1. How do I react if my spouse asks me to do something I don't want to do? How can I honor God in that circumstance?

2. Why does God ask us to honor all people?

3. What are some ways I can submit to my spouse? For example, who is stronger in dealing with family finances? Can we allow that person's strength to handle that particular situation as the other submits?

4. Am I seeking godly counsel or worldly advice? If I am seeking worldly advice, is there someone I can trust to provide Christian counseling and help me seek God's Word on the subject? *(Note: You must be willing to listen, and then you must submit and obey when you hear godly counseling or receive a word from the Lord.)*

5. Is my marriage on hold or headed toward divorce because of pride? *(For example, are there things you are not willing to do to save your marriage, such as not being willing to stop hanging out with your friends or not being willing to change because you think the other person should change? Has that become more important to you than honoring Christ in your marriage?)*

Developing Character

Continually look for ways you can practice submission at home, work, and church. For example, if your wife enjoys romantic movies and you do not, rent a movie or take her to a movie and enjoy it anyway. If your husband enjoys sports, buy tickets to a game or watch a game on television with him. If you have a particular place you like to sit in church but the ushers want you to sit elsewhere, follow their leading. Or if your boss tells you to write a report that may be outside your job description, submit and do it anyway.

Affirmation

I will trust in the Lord with all my heart. I will not lean on my own understanding. I will acknowledge him, and he shall direct my path.

Reflections

_____

_____

_____

_____

_____

_____

_____

_____

_____

_____

_____

_____

_____

_____

5

Prick Your Finger

To Die Is to Live

I am crucified with Christ: nevertheless I live; yet not I, but Christ liveth in me: and the life which I now live in the flesh I live by the faith of the Son of God, who loved me, and gave himself for me.

Galatians 2:20

Just pause and think about the Scripture passage above. What does it mean to you? Paul describes the death that must take place in his flesh in order for him to do what God had called him to do. Likewise, this death allows Christ to be seen in all of us and allows him to work through us. In the Sleeping Beauty fairy tale, the princess pricked her finger on the spinning wheel; yet though she was thought to be dead, she was still alive. Dying to our flesh means that though we yet live, we die. Although it may be a painful experience at the time, it is really just a decision to allow God

149

to increase in your life. This death may hurt for a moment, but by God's grace, it will not kill you.

Denying Self

I now understand that my life is no longer my own, especially when it comes to my marriage, because I have accepted Jesus into my life. Jesus said, "If any person wills to come after Me, let him deny himself [disown himself, forget, lose sight of himself and his own interests, refuse and give up himself] and take up his cross daily and follow Me [cleave steadfastly to Me, conform wholly to My example in living and, if need be, in dying also]" (Luke 9:23 AMP). In order to fulfill God's will for our lives, we must decrease and allow him to increase in us (see John 3:30). That cross Jesus is referring to will *hurt* when you pick it up and begin to follow the Lord. It will cost you something to take up your cross and follow his ways—sacrifice, unconditional love, forgiveness, submission, and more. Letting go of who you are now in order to be who God wants you to be is not an easy thing, but in the end is a blessing—a promise to those who hold on and continue to follow the Lord no matter how tough things may get. In order to follow Jesus, a death must take place. This death allows Jesus to be seen in our lives by others. It is a death by which a person accepts a higher calling (or as others would say, the higher road) in order to grow and mature in the things of God.

After Lewis and I separated and I was desperately seeking God for answers, the Lord told me to go to John 19:18, which reads, "They crucified him, and two other with him, on either side one, and Jesus in the midst."

I knew that two robbers died with Jesus, but God said, "No, look at them as sinners. Put your husband on one side and you on the other."

I said, "Okay, now what?"

He said, "Die."

How do we do that? By doing everything opposite of what our flesh tells us. For example, if Lewis asks me to cook and I don't want to, but I do it anyway, that brings me closer to the cross. Or when I am arguing with him and the Holy Spirit tells me to shut up, and I do it, that brings me closer to the cross. Or if I am acting foolishly and the Holy Spirit tells Lewis to bless me, and he does, it brings him closer to the cross. By the time both husband and wife die to self, they will truly become one.

Daily means that it is a continuing process. Your flesh is never dead until you die a physical death, so you must work on killing its desires every day. No, you don't physically kill yourself. It is a fleshly death whereby your spirit is in control, not your flesh. Some people call it willpower while others call it self-discipline or self-control.

self-control: the ability to deny yourself, control your impulses, exhibit self-discipline, and rein in your behavior

You must deny what you want, what you feel, and what you think when it is contrary to God's will. Before Jesus died, he prayed for God to remove the cup (what he was about to face), yet he wanted not his will but God's will to be done. Jesus understood that his assignment on the earth was never about what he wanted, what he felt, or what he thought. He only wanted to do what was right in the sight of God. In marriage, when you die to your flesh, you accept the cup (all the things your spouse does that you don't like and all the things your spouse asks you to do that you don't want to do) and allow God's will, not your will, to be done in your marriage. For example, I have one way of handling things and Lewis has another. I can't stand his ways. To me, they don't allow me to be who I am. But God is showing me a bigger vision, and if I deny my own perception of myself in order to unite to that vision, all will be well. In the business we run, God is the CEO and Lewis is the president. When I keep my eyes on the CEO, I can deny my own desires more easily than if I think Lewis is the one in charge. However, I have determined that for the success of our company and the glory that God wants to get from it, I must unite to the vision God gave Lewis. By uniting biblically to one single (God-given) vision, we now have a successful company.

Here are some examples of denying your own desires:

1. Deny what you think.
   - If God tells your spouse to ask you to quit your job and stay at home to raise your children, just do it. Also, husbands, if your wife asks you to complete a "honey do" list, then work on it and finish the tasks. Trust God, knowing that his grace is sufficient.
   - Let go of your pet peeves. (So what if he doesn't seal the bag in the cereal box? *You* do it.)
2. Deny what you want.
   - Depart from sin: smoking, drinking, drugs, and sex outside of marriage.
   - Deny your plans, goals, and aspirations, and seek God's plans for your life.
3. Deny what you feel.
   - If your spouse wants dinner, cook. If your spouse wants sex, make love.
   - Help and give to others, even when you think you don't have the time.

It takes just one person in the marriage to be committed, to stay in the Word, and to work toward a heavenly marriage for it to stay somewhat peaceful. Why? Because when one person is in the flesh and the other remains in the Spirit, both aren't acting like fools. The one being led by the Holy Spirit can bring stability, encouragement, and growth to the relationship because that partner is continuing to grow spiritually—he or she is building their inner (spiritual) man. Praying, praise and worship, reading the Word, and fellowshiping with God will help to build your spirit to be stronger than your flesh.

As you continue to grow, being able to deny what you think, feel, and want becomes much easier. As Paul wrote, "I am crucified with Christ: nevertheless I live; yet not I, but Christ liveth in me: and the life which I now live in the flesh I live by the faith of the Son of God, who loved me, and gave himself for me" (Gal. 2:20).

Our marriages are to be patterned after Christ's love for the church. First John 3:16 says, "Hereby perceive we the love of God, because he laid down his life for us: and we ought to lay down our lives for the brethren." Because of Jesus's love for the church, he gave of himself (died); and because he was resurrected, we too can die to who we used to be so that our lives and marriages can live again. Why is it that we can die to our selfish ways when we have children or get a job, but we have trouble when it comes to our spouses? When you have a baby, you die to your flesh because life becomes all about the baby's needs and not yours. When the baby awakes at midnight, 3:00 a.m., and 6:00 a.m., you must get up. When you get a job, you die to what you want and you do what is necessary to keep that job. Some of us have to get up at 4:00 a.m. just to get to work on time. But when it comes to the very gift God has given us—our husband or wife—we are selfish and refuse to change.

Dying to your flesh (daily laying aside your own desires)

- allows God to order your steps,
- helps you to walk in the image and likeness of God,
- helps you to think of others and not yourself,
- means you're walking in the Spirit, and
- keeps you from sinning.

If you are not dying to your flesh,

- you stay a lover of yourself rather than a lover of God,
- you stay wise in your own eyes rather than trusting God,
- you are selfish,

- your flesh will lead to sin, and
- you dishonor God.

After looking at the benefits of dying to your flesh versus not dying to your flesh, it is obvious to see which will enable you to build a stronger loving marriage that pleases God. Moreover, when making that decision to die to your flesh, you will find that problems will not mount up into irreconcilable differences.

Reconcilable Differences

The reason most often cited for marriages ending in divorce is "irreconcilable differences." Every time I hear that term, I get a little upset because I wonder what those differences are. Is it a difference of opinions? A difference in beliefs? Yes, the Bible says we are to become one, but it does not state that we are to become the *same*. We should embrace the differences in each other because where one may be weak, the other may be strong. Your mate's strengths should cover your weaknesses. The result is that you are strong together as a couple, and you lack nothing between the two of you. For example, I love researching and purchasing investment opportunities, but I am not good at keeping track of the money that was spent. Lewis, on the other hand, tracks everything (and I mean *everything*). We argue so much over why I have to keep records the way he does because I think it's crazy and time-consuming. But my weakness is made strong since Lewis keeps track of everything and expects it from me. Therefore, not only is Lewis bringing out the best in me, but with both of us using the skills we have, he is also strengthening our finances.

Ironically, I can almost guarantee that the very thing that attracted you to your spouse may be the very thing that gets on your nerves now that you are married. Again, I love the fact that my husband tracks his spending and keeps his checkbook up to date. I know that our finances will always be okay because Lewis is so great with money. But I do not like that he tracks *my* spending and that he adds me to his tracking list of "people who owe me money"!

Don't get me wrong. We argued a lot about our differences until we finally figured out how to handle them appropriately. The key to disagreeing is to not become destructive and tear one another down but to find a place of agreement after voicing your concerns. I remember one time that Lewis and I had a big argument because he was going through some health issues. He came to me upset because he didn't feel as though I was doing a great job taking care of him. "You don't care what's going on with me," he complained. "Did you research to see what was going on?" My response was, "No, I didn't," and I told him to leave me alone. After praying about it, I realized that what Lewis wanted me to do for him was what *he* would have done for me. It is not what *I* would do. He has to respect the fact that I am not one who would research health issues as he does, just as he doesn't research investment opportunities as I do. I asked him not to get upset with me because I don't handle things his way and vice versa. If he had wanted me to research it for him, he should have told me so, and I would have done it.

In each set of circumstances, we cannot expect our spouses to react the way we would or do the same thing we would do. What is obvious to one may not be obvious to the other. We were all brought up under different rules and conditions. Lewis grew up poor, and I didn't. Therefore, we have differences of opinions on some things, but we make adjustments for one another while still maintaining our beliefs and values. It's called compromise. Let go of preconceived ideas and family rules that you were taught. Now that you are married, it is time for you to set new traditions for *your* family. Embrace your differences and use them to your advantage and not for your demise. Knowing your spouse and being flexible are key to having a great marriage.

Successful couples understand that it is okay to have different opinions and ways of doing things because they are able to use what

God has given them for his glory. They know how to submit to one another and allow the strengths of one to cover the weaknesses of the other.

United as One

The goal in marriage is not for two people to become the same. It is for them to become *one*. Uniting in purpose to do what God is calling you to do is going to be a challenge. Paul tells us in Romans 12:4–8 that we all have different gifts, talents, and qualities and to use them accordingly. However, we are one in body and purpose, and each is mutually dependent upon the other. As a couple, you have to discover each other's talents and abilities and know how to work them into your marriage. For example, say you are a person who is very organized and your spouse is not. Instead of trying to change your spouse to be more like you, take on the responsibility of keeping both your appointments and your spouse's up-to-date. A couple that understands how they complement one another is a couple that will have a very successful marriage.

Couples can become one in spirit, soul, and body. When you get married, pray continually that your spirits always line up with one another. "Can two walk together, except they be agreed?" (Amos 3:3). To be united in spirit with our spouses means being agreeable, sympathetic, compassionate, and humble.

> **unite:** to bring together in a common purpose or endeavor

Couples can unite spiritually. They can pray together. They can come into agreement concerning marriage, finances, or business. Couples also become one when they walk in unconditional love. Our desire should be living to please God, which ultimately helps us to esteem our spouses more highly than ourselves (see Phil. 2:3).

I ask the Holy Spirit daily what I should do concerning Lewis, our children, and our family business. I ask God to speak to him and to me so that we are in agreement about all things.

God is no respecter of persons. Just as he sent angels to speak to Joseph and Mary about the name of their son Jesus (see Matt. 1:21 and Luke 1:31), he can speak to you daily concerning what you need to know about one another. It is also important to recognize that if you are the wife, God will speak to your man of God as well as to you. God is the Father of order and decency. He told Mary that she would be pregnant with a child not of Joseph, but he told Joseph before she did. He also continued speaking to Joseph instead of Mary concerning what Joseph should do regarding his family (see Matthew 1–2). She just had to follow her man of God.

In order to become one in soul (mind, will, and emotions), couples must renew their minds with what the Word of God says concerning their marriage; understand and fulfill the will of God for their marriage; allow shared interests and experiences to bring them closer; and respect one another's differences, including opinions, behaviors, and personalities.

Becoming one in body is to deny the flesh—the natural desires. To deny the flesh is to resist all the appetites of the flesh (see Gal. 5:17–19). Intimacy is a big part of becoming one. Successful relationships have openness, romance, sex, and daily doses of love. The goal in marriage is oneness—that the two shall become one (see Eph. 5:31).

oneness: when two different people have come together under one God-given vision and are now working together as a unit to achieve that vision for common purposes and goals

Ephesians 4:4–6 says, "You were all called to travel on the same road and in the same direction, so stay together, both outwardly and inwardly. You have one Master, one faith, one baptism, one

God and Father of all, who rules over all, works through all, and is present in all. Everything you are and think and do is permeated with Oneness" (Message). Finding ways to become one is key to a successful, growing relationship. You will never reach the fullness of God's love and purpose for your lives as a couple until you attain oneness with one another, which is found in him.

I have identified five things that will stop you from becoming one as a couple:

1. Unforgiveness
2. Hardness of heart
3. Disagreements
4. Selfishness
5. Violating trust

If any of these apply to you, repent and ask God to show you how to correct the area that has been stopping you from becoming one with your spouse. Here are some things you can do to help you and your mate become closer:

1. Ask your mate to tell you one thing you can do for him or her this week (nothing sexual).
2. Plan one day a month or even a week of doing anything and everything that will please your mate (don't tell him or her what you are going to do or when you're going to do it).
3. Pray for God to reveal something about your mate that day, listen to the Lord's voice, and do it. (For example, your spouse may be thinking, "It sure would be nice to have lunch at my favorite restaurant," and God may tell you to call him or her for a lunch date.)
4. Give your spouse the day off (men cook and take care of the children one evening, or women let your husband come home and rest with dinner in bed).

5. Acknowledge your spouse and praise them daily for the little things.
6. Always look at one another through God's eyes.

Equally Yoked

To be equally yoked with one another is to understand why you are united in the first place. What is your purpose? Why has God joined the two of you together? All marriages have a purpose. Know that God usually brings equals together, which means that both individuals bring something to the marriage that God can use in a mighty way. He takes the strengths of one to cover the weaknesses of another. That is why both are to submit one to another; one who is weak in one area should submit to the other who is strong in that area. That is why you should not look at or talk about the weaknesses of your mate. Your strength covers that person's weakness, and that is how you can elevate them. You might have thought that meeting your spouse was just coincidental—something about them pleased you. I don't think so! Nothing just happens. God knew with whom, when, why, and how you were going to come together. Again, it's not about you; it's about God's plan for you as a couple.

In God's sight, a husband and wife are one. Therefore, God's plan and purpose for your lives is a joint venture. The two of you need one another to complete the plan. Most marriages fail to realize or unite in their purpose because spouses never see themselves as united as one but still see themselves as separate individuals. Two married individuals should complement one another like two interlocking circles.

> **complement:** something that completes, makes up a whole, or brings to perfection

In the following diagram, the part that is shaded is where you have become one. For example, you both agree that you want your marriage to succeed. The more you start dying to the flesh, the more you will move toward oneness, as illustrated by the shaded part of the two circles.

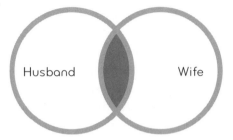

If you are not married yet, find that common denominator between you and your fiancé. Ask yourself, "How could God use us?" In 2 Corinthians 6:14, Paul says, "Do not be unequally yoked with unbelievers [do not make mismated alliances with them or come under a different yoke with them, inconsistent with your faith]" (AMP). For the most part, this verse is about believers and non-believers. For example, a Christian marrying a Muslim would be unequally yoked. But it also means that both individuals should be equal in other things as well.

For example, a woman who loves to wear mink coats more than likely should not marry an animal activist. They are unequally yoked. God is a God of order and decency, and he always puts equals together. So two people who both have an interest in animals should be together, and that is how God can use their marriage as a ministry. If you look at most successful couples, they have something in common. Take a look at couples who are called by God in specific ways. The majority of the time, if he has been called into the ministry, she has too. As another example, my husband and I both have entrepreneurial minds. Ever since I was in elementary school, I have wanted to own my own business. When Lewis and I met, he stated that his desire was to have a business too. I didn't realize it at first, but that is one of the reasons God put us together—to have a business ministry.

When we separated and I was seeking God for answers, he said that my marriage was out of order. My thought was that Antiok Holdings Inc. was Lewis's business and his vision, and I had to get my own. But God told me no, it was God's vision, and I was called to be a helpmeet for God's business. That was one reason Lewis and I were together. I was trying to start a business at the same time Antiok was taking off, and Lewis really needed my help. God now has us ministering to high school students who are interested in starting a business.

As a couple, we are living epistles for Christ. Those children and others should see Christ in us when we are working together. Your marriage is not just a marriage; it is a ministry through which people can get a glimpse of Jesus without us opening the Bible or giving Scripture verses. That is why it is important to be equally yoked as a couple in mind, body, and spirit.

This is not to say that couples can't have two businesses (or ministries), but one may have to be put on hold for a while if God has called you to help your spouse. Ministry should never separate a couple or cause them to be in competition with one another. That is not God's plan. God needs us (Christians) to fulfill his plan, which is to save souls. But everything must be done decently and in order. How can a wife be a helpmeet if she doesn't know or experience what her husband does? I believe that is why you see so many husband and wife teams in the ministry today. God put those two individuals together because they are equally yoked in their calling. Eve was created so she could help Adam tend the garden. Most successful couples work in the same career field, enjoy the same types of activities (photography, mountain climbing), or have the same interests (helping homeless people, animal activism).

What do you and your mate have in common? If you don't know, ask your spouse about his or her dreams and interests. Above all, ask God what his plans and purposes are for your marriage. As Paul urges us, "Then make my joy complete by being like-minded, having the same love, being one in spirit and purpose" (Phil. 2:2 NIV). The main common denominator you have as a Christian couple is that you both love God and are committed to serving and fulfilling his plan for your life.

In order to fulfill your purpose, you must develop a relationship with your heavenly Father. Just as you talk to those whom you desire to know, talk to God every day and ask questions. Trust me, he will answer every one of them. You can start by asking, "Is my home (or family) a place where God dwells?" God wants to hear from you about every aspect of your life. He wants to lead you to the good life and down the right path. Find your common ground as a couple. I assure you that when you do and when you start working together, your marriage will flourish and become all God has called it to be.

The Bible tells us of a couple, Priscilla and Aquila, whose purpose was to establish churches. They both were tentmakers (they were equally yoked), and they opened their home as a meeting place. Both were well versed in the Word of God and helped people understand it. Their story in Acts 18 is short and sweet, but God wants you to see that everyone has a purpose. Theirs may not have been mighty in deed, but God was pleased with what they did. Will you be faithful in your ministry at home? Do you show the love of Jesus to your spouse and children? Or do they just see it on Sundays at church? Your family is your first ministry. Once you are successful in that, God will move you to do other things.

Unite Biblically

Uniting biblically will help a couple to become one, which is the foundational principle for marriage. It will also help them learn how to become true followers of Christ. But ultimately, it will help a couple understand and fulfill their purpose. Proverbs 29:18 states, "Where there is no vision [no redemptive revelation of God], the people perish; but he who keeps the law [of God, which includes that of man]—blessed (happy, fortunate, and enviable) is he" (AMP). Marriages are being destroyed because couples haven't caught the vision God has for them. But as for those who obey God and his commandments, they will be happy. As you seek God and his kingdom, his vision for your life will be revealed.

In John 21, Jesus asked Peter three times if he loved him. Peter got angry at first and then said, "Jesus, you know all things. Yes, I love you" (see John 21:17 NIV). Then Jesus said, "'I tell you the truth, when you were younger you dressed yourself and went where you wanted; but when you are old you will stretch out your hands, and someone else will dress you and lead you where you do not want to go.' Jesus said this to indicate the kind of death by which Peter would glorify God. Then he said to him, 'Follow me!'" (vv. 18–19 NIV). Ultimately, God is trying to get us to a place where we die to who we are to become who we are in Christ. Then we become true followers of Jesus. You cannot become a true follower until you have displayed Christlike characteristics.

All the biblical couples I have talked about in this book (with the exception of King Ahasuerus and Vashti) understood their purpose and aligned themselves to that vision. Some probably didn't understand why God wanted them to do things a particular way, but they submitted to his will anyway. You may not understand why God wants you to do what he has called you to do, but if you want to fulfill God's will for your life, seek him, and when his will is revealed, *do it!* A person or couple who *unites biblically* understands that they have purpose, and they are willing to fulfill that purpose together.

Prayer

Dear Lord God, I recognize that you created me as a unique individual, yet you have called me to be united and to be in harmony with my spouse. You have called us to work alongside one another for your purpose, and in walking in unity, we will fulfill your ultimate plan for our lives as a couple. Thank you, Lord, that where one is weak, the other is strong. Help us to recognize areas where we can complement one another and not tear one another down. I declare and decree unity in our home, marriage, finances, and child rearing. Thank you for the Word, the truth—that I may be set free to do your will. Father, not my will but your will be done in our lives from this day forward. Now, in the name of Jesus, I decree and declare that my flesh is no longer on the throne, and I now live by the Spirit of God. In Jesus's name, amen.

For a free copy of the article "Seven Steps toward Financial Freedom," visit www.marriage101.us.

ALTR**U**ISM:
Unite Biblically

> A great marriage is not when the "perfect couple" comes together. It is when an imperfect couple learns to enjoy their differences.
>
> Dave Meurer

To *unite biblically*, you need to understand the differences between you and your mate and how those differences can be used for God's glory. Blending differences and learning how to become one in purpose will create challenges and tests. These challenges will either make you stronger or break down the union. The goal of this section is to help you, as a couple, find your common purpose, accept your different behaviors and ways, and unite in purpose to fulfill the call of God on your lives as a married couple. *Uniting biblically* brings you and your spouse into agreement concerning the purpose God has for your marriage.

Biblical Example: Aquila and Priscilla (Acts 18)

This couple's story is short but sweet. This outstanding husband and wife team became one by using their God-given skills and their home to do great work for the Lord. Throughout the Scriptures you will always see their names listed together (see also Rom. 16:3–5; 1 Cor. 16:19; 2 Tim. 4:19). They were a couple who understood their purpose as a couple. They were equally yoked in talent and ministry. They both had the same occupation (tentmaker) and used it as a way to support themselves. They were united in purpose and became teachers and evangelists of the gospel by traveling and holding church meetings in their home. Their hospitality to others led many to salvation. Look how God can use a willing couple! An ordinary couple can do extraordinary things for the gospel if they make themselves available for God to use.

No matter what weaknesses you think you have, no matter what state your marriage is in, God can use you. This couple decided to use what they had and committed themselves to God and the work he predestined for them. One way to find victory in a situation is to bless others who may be going through the same thing. Just praying for someone's health, for example, may help you get a breakthrough in your own health. Giving to the poor may help you gain personal prosperity. For me, when I decided to be a part of the vision God had given Lewis, our business took off. I had been the holdup. We were not united in purpose—God's purpose. Therefore, in the beginning, our business did not flourish as fast as it could have. It was a slow—very slow—process to get to where we are today.

Scripture Meditation

Meditate on the following Scriptures to understand how to *unite biblically* and the sacrifice it will take to become one. Ask God to show you why you and your spouse should unite biblically for his purpose. Write down anything God reveals to you in the space after each verse.

Mark 10:8–9 (AMP)

"And the two shall become one flesh, so that they are no longer two, but one flesh. What therefore God has united (joined together), let not man separate or divide."

_____

_____

_____

_____

_____

Philippians 2:2 (AMP)

"Fill up and complete my joy by living in harmony and being of the same mind and one in purpose, having the same love, being in full accord and of one harmonious mind and intention."

_____

_____

_____

_____

_____

Luke 9:23–25 (Message)

"Then he [Jesus] told them what they could expect for themselves: 'Anyone who intends to come with me has to let me lead. You're not in the driver's seat—I am. Don't run from suffering; embrace it. Follow me and I'll show you how. Self-help is no help at all. Self-sacrifice is the way, my way, to finding yourself, your true self. What good would it do to get everything you want and lose you, the real you?'"

_____

_____

_____

_____

Philippians 1:27 (Message)

"Meanwhile, live in such a way that you are a credit to the Message of Christ. Let nothing in your conduct hang on whether I come or not. Your conduct must be the same whether I show up to see things for myself or hear of it from a distance. Stand united, singular in vision, contending for people's trust in the Message, the good news."

_____

_____

_____

_____

Amos 3:3 (Message)

"Do two people walk hand in hand if they aren't going to the same place?"

_____

_____

_____

_____

_____

Self-Examination

1. If my marriage could be represented by two overlapping circles, how large would our overlapping area be? In what areas have my spouse and I become one thus far? What can I do to move us closer to becoming one? For example, perhaps the two of you are raising children, yet you have not decided how they should be disciplined or have not communicated about how

they should be raised (for example, not being able to watch certain television programs, etc.).

2. In what ways are my spouse and I different? How can we blend those differences to have a positive outcome in our marriage and be united in purpose?

3. What weaknesses and strengths do we each bring to our marriage (for example, finance, business, raising children, etc.)?

My weaknesses:

My strengths:

My spouse's weaknesses:

My spouse's strengths:

4. Now combine the list. How do you cover one another? Use this information to help you decide what roles each should play in the household. For example, your strength may be giving, while your spouse's strength may be managing money, so you both can now agree on the roles and do your part of the task.

5. What is the one thing you can do that will help bring the two of you closer?

Developing Character

One way for couples to work toward building unity in their marriage is to find a common cause or goal and work together at achieving it. For example, identify a project, hobby, ministry at church that you would enjoy doing together. Sign up and see it through until completion. Remember, you are working on building unity in your relationship, so focus on points of agreement rather than disagreement when undertaking your new commitment together.

Affirmation

Today I make a commitment to reconcile any differences that my spouse and I may have so we can unite as one. Together we will fulfill God's plan and purpose for our lives.

Reflections

6

Deep Sleep

Repent! It Is Time to Change

Awake thou that sleepest, and arise from the dead, and Christ shall give thee light.

Ephesians 5:14

In February 2001, I was having my wilderness experience. I thought attending a marriage conference was my last resort for saving my marriage. By the end of the conference, I realized that I was a wife out of position and out of control. My thoughts, my actions, and my words were not in line with the Word of God. I realized that I was a hearer of the Word but not a doer of the Word.

On the very first day of the conference, God dealt with me about the following: (1) order regarding my family, (2) sex in my marriage, (3) excuses for not doing what I knew was right, (4) unforgiveness, and (5) actions and words I was sowing into my marriage. For years, Lewis and I had no clue as to God's plan and purpose for our marriage, so our marriage was in deep trouble. We had no idea that it could be great, but it would require a lot of work.

Christian marriages are in trouble because we do not know or understand God's plan for marriage, especially as it relates to our own. Just as the evil fairy cursed the princess and put her into a deep sleep until her true love kissed her, we too will continue to be in a deep sleep until we get a revelation of what Jesus has done for us, change our behavior, and fulfill our purpose as a married couple.

The Wilderness Experience

Every marriage will have a wilderness experience—a time when you will be tested and tempted by the enemy. The hardest thing you will ever do is go through that rough period and make it to the other side to experience victory. The road to the other side will be different for every couple, based on the choices they make. Some couples may only need to assume their proper roles (as discussed in chapter 2). Others may have to forgive the sins of their spouse and deal with their own sins. This was big for us because Lewis carried a grudge against me in his heart for years. Once the issue was discussed and I apologized, we were on our way toward reconciliation. To see the glory of God in your marriage will require you to change. It will require you to forgive. It will require you to love unconditionally. And it will require you to spend much time with God.

Have you ever wondered why people can date for years and get married but then get divorced within one year? How is it that you put up with your spouse's faults and those little pet peeves while you were dating, but once you got married, they became monumental issues and problems that you now can't seem to deal with? Why is the enemy after marriages? Why does the enemy hate marriages so much that they are attacked immediately until they are destroyed? The enemy has not changed. He attacked the very first

Deep Sleep

marriage, that of Adam and Eve, from the very beginning. Why? Because God has blessed each couple to be like him—to be fruitful, to multiply, and to replenish and have dominion over the entire earth. We are to use all of the resources God has given us to serve God and man (see Gen. 1:26–28). However, the enemy is looking for us to serve him.

You may be going through a rough time in your marriage right now. You may be feeling as if you are in a dark place and believing the only way to escape the pain, heartache, or problem is to divorce. I know because that is exactly how I felt when my relationship had reached an all-time low. Right after I kicked Lewis out of the house, I was trying to convince myself that I had done all I could to save my marriage. I felt that our struggles were Lewis's fault for not trying hard enough, but God revealed that I was part of the problem. He told me that I was a wife out of position and out of control. I was making excuses as to why I couldn't be a good wife because, in my eyes, Lewis wasn't a godly husband.

My thoughts and actions did not line up with what I had been taught about marriage from the Bible. I had to stop blaming my husband for our failing relationship because I was partly responsible, even though I didn't think so at the time. Even though my husband had given his life to Jesus, he was not interested in living a Christian lifestyle. He was simply in a backslidden state. Therefore, it was my responsibility, as the one who was open to hearing from God, to start the process of change. If I wanted God to intervene on behalf of my marriage, I had to repent and change my behavior. Once my eyes were opened, I began to renew my mind concerning God's will for my marriage by aligning my thoughts with his Word.

It is easy to lose sight of the good in your spouse when things are going wrong, but look to Jesus and always keep him in the forefront of your mind. He will give perfect peace to those whose minds are focused on him (see Isa. 26:3). Keeping your mind on Jesus is just doing what Jesus would do. For example, when Jesus was in the wilderness, he was hungry and alone while being tempted by Satan (see Matt. 4:1–11). Jesus was tempted:

- physically—because he hadn't eaten for forty days
- mentally—Satan questioned his true identity
- emotionally—Satan made appeals to his pride

God's Word says that we will be tempted, but it is not of him. Satan tempts us:

- mentally—(1) by sowing doubts, such as, "You married the wrong person" or "There is no hope for your marriage"; (2) by telling us lies, "You can handle a particular temptation"; (3) by distorting our perception, "a married man/woman appearing to be available but they are not"
- emotionally—by keeping us focused on the problems
- physically—by convincing us that there are no boundaries and that sexual temptation is okay. God gave Adam and Eve everything but one tree to eat from (boundaries), and Satan said, "No, you can eat from all the trees."

Read the passage below and see how the enemy worked in Adam and Eve's circumstances:

Now the serpent was more cunning than any beast of the field which the LORD God had made. And he said to the woman, "Has God indeed said, 'You shall not eat of every tree of the garden'?" And the woman said to the serpent, "We may eat the fruit of the trees of the garden; but of the fruit of the tree which *is* in the midst of the garden, God has said, 'You shall not eat it, nor shall you touch it, lest you die.'" Then the serpent said to the woman, "You will not surely die. For God knows that in the day you eat of it your eyes will be opened, and you will be like God, knowing good and evil." So when the woman saw that the tree *was* good for food, that it *was* pleasant to the eyes, and a tree desirable to make *one* wise, she took of its fruit and ate. She also gave to her husband with her, and he ate.

Genesis 3:1–6 NKJV

The enemy doesn't change. He will tempt you at your weakest point. Do not flirt with temptation. If and when you are being tempted, pray for strength. Override the temptation by using God's Word to cast that evil thought away. Look for a way of escape because God always provides one (see 1 Cor. 10:13). Do not add fuel to the fire by flirting with temptation or trying to convince yourself you can handle what is going on.

I don't think I'm going out on a limb to say that all marriages will have a wilderness experience. Marriages will be tested, tried, and put through the fire. But you have to recognize those times for what they are—just a trial. First Peter 4:12–13 says, "Beloved, think it not strange concerning the fiery trial which is to try you, as though some strange thing happened unto you: But rejoice, inasmuch as ye are partakers of Christ's sufferings; that, when his glory shall be revealed, ye may be glad also with exceeding joy."

Jesus was able to defeat the enemy by dying on the cross for our sins. He is our prime example: "Looking unto Jesus the author and finisher of our faith: who for the joy that was set before him endured the cross, despising the shame, and is set down at the right hand of the throne of God" (Heb. 12:2). There is a joy that is set before you in your marriage if you can just find a way to receive it. I can honestly say that God's Word is true and my marriage is so much better now that I have gone through my test and found victory on the other side.

Even though our suffering will not be anything like Jesus's, we can praise God that on the other end of it is joy. But you must go through this wilderness experience in order to receive your reward from God. My test brought me closer to God: it helped me to develop character; it allowed me to help others as I witnessed the goodness of God and how his Word is true; it gave me the opportunity to glorify God because of what he had done in my marriage; and I defeated the enemy! I am so much better for having gone through the fire. And you will be too.

In the book of Job, Satan answered God, "Does Job [reverently] fear God for nothing? Have You not put a hedge about him and his house and all that he has, on every side? You have conferred prosperity and happiness upon him in the work of his hands, and his possessions have increased in the land. But put forth your hand now and touch all that he has, and he will curse You to Your face" (Job 1:9–11 AMP). Because Satan hasn't changed, I believe he is still doing this today—trying to get us to curse God. Even Job's wife told him to curse God and die, but Job held on to his righteousness and his relationship with God. In the end, Job received back double of everything he had lost. Do not curse God during your test, but allow that experience to bring you closer to him. God is waiting to have a relationship with you.

You can't change external situations (such as your marriage) if you don't change internally in your mind and thoughts. The enemy will always have you focus on the negatives—faults, bad behavior, or differences in personalities. However, we should focus on the positive things concerning our mates. Philippians 4:8 says, "Finally, brethren, whatsoever things are true, whatsoever things are honest, whatsoever things are just, whatsoever things are pure, whatsoever things are lovely, whatsoever things are of good report; if there be any virtue, and if there be any praise, think on these things." I used to focus so much on the fact that my husband wasn't going to church. In my mind, he was a heathen. I became self-righteous in my thinking. I thought that I was better (in other words, more spiritual) than he was, and I started desiring to be married to someone else—a churchgoing man. I had to repent and change my outlook on my husband. He just hadn't reached the fullness of what God had planned for his life, but he is working on it now. Again, when God starts to show you *your* faults, you will realize that you are not all that you think you are!

Decency and Order

The apostle Paul gave the Corinthian church some instructions that reveal the nature of God: "God is not the author of confusion, but of peace. . . . [So] let all things be done decently and in order" (1 Cor. 14:33, 40). You can apply the same instructions to your life and your marriage. We should follow a specific order to avoid confusion and promote peace in our families. Some claim this isn't biblical; however, it is based on 1 Corinthians 11:3 and Ephesians 6:1. That order that God ordained is as follows:

1. God
2. Jesus
3. Man
4. Woman
5. Children
6. Ministry (church activities)

When you get married, the two of you become one flesh. Then, when you have children, you produce a godly seed. But notice that God never says in his Word to cleave to your children. They are God's responsibility (he ultimately is their provider through you), and your job is to love them and train them in the way they should go (see Prov. 22:6). Ephesians 6:4 says, "Fathers, provoke not your children to wrath: but bring them up in the nurture and admonition of the Lord." Those children are not yours. God is just using you as a vessel to bring them into the world and raise them to be men and women of God. Jesus wasn't Mary's to hold on to either. Her job was just to love and train him.

All this is to say that, women, you cannot put your children before your husband. That is out of order. Just as you would never put your husband before God, so you must not put your children before your man of God. Now some of you might be saying, "I have to take care of my kids. They can't take care of themselves," or "They are blood and he's not," or "He could leave one day, but my kids will always be with me." I used to say the same things, and God had to work with me on this issue. If you rationalize that your husband could leave or that his blood doesn't run through your veins, you have not entered into the type of marriage God has ordained. Your husband is bone of your bone and flesh of your flesh; you two have become one, which is closer than anything on this earth, including a parent and child.

Just think, God says you are to "cleave" to your spouse (Gen. 2:24). *Cleave* in the Greek is *kollao*, which comes from the Greek word *kolla*, which means "glue." If you glue anything together—like wallpaper to a wall or paper to paper—and try to tear it apart, you'll get a piece left on the other. You cannot completely tear apart something that is glued together. That is how God intended marriage to be. You cannot completely separate from your husband. A part of him is always with you. However, God says that a man (your son) should *leave* (not cleave to) his mother and father (see Matt. 19:5). God says that children will leave and should separate themselves from their parents. If you have a son, he must leave his parents and cleave to his wife, and he and his wife will become one; your daughter must leave you and cleave to her husband. With the new couple, God starts another church family (a place where God dwells).

Please understand that the husband and wife are lifetime partners. They build a foundation before any children come. When children arrive, the couple has about eighteen years to train them, and then the children move into adulthood to start their own families. During this time, the couple must still maintain a level of commitment toward one another. They cannot allow the children to shift their focus so that they lose sight of one another. Remember, your children are going to leave at some point. You and your spouse are still a family when they are gone. Is your house in order?

I also made the mistake of putting ministry before my family. I would go to church meetings and wouldn't fix dinner. So my husband would come home, after working all day, to no meal. Yes, his hands worked just fine and he could have fixed his own meal, but per our agreement, cooking dinner was my responsibility. On Bible study nights, I would stop at a fast-food restaurant, and the kids would eat on their way to church. That was wrong! I was so concerned about what I needed to do for the church and what I thought God wanted me to do for the church that I wasn't actually doing what was pleasing to him. I wasn't taking care of my number one ministry: the family God gave me. It is important that we find a balance in all we do without jeopardizing our families.

Sex in Marriage

In 1 Corinthians, Paul gives this advice regarding marital relations: "Do not deprive each other except by mutual consent and for a time, so that you may devote yourselves to prayer. Then come together again so that Satan will not tempt you because of your lack of self-control" (1 Cor. 7:5 NIV). Sex is a vital, God-given part of your marriage relationship. Instead of thinking of it as an act or even calling it "sex," think of it as you and your husband ministering to one another.

Why do we have problems in our marriages regarding sex? The answer is selfishness. We don't consider the other's needs. Are you the type of person who only has sex when you are interested? Lewis and I had to find a balance in our sex life because I am a morning person, and he is an evening person. We had to talk about it and make a commitment to meet one another's needs, even if that meant compromising on exactly what each of us wants for ourselves. It really boils down to this: is your marriage worth keeping, or would you rather not compromise and risk your spouse having an affair to get his or her needs met? I am not saying this to put anyone in bondage but am saying it based on 1 Corinthians 7:5.

If you are having sex only once a month or less, you may have a problem in your marriage (unless you have health needs or physical problems that prohibit it or this is the frequency you and your spouse are comfortable with). A lack of intimacy in your relationship can be a door for sin to enter and destroy your marriage, especially if one of you is feeling consistently frustrated, deprived, lonely, or unloved. So communicate with your spouse about your needs and desires. And remember to show your affection often. Kiss your spouse. Don't just give a quick, thoughtless peck as you're on your way out the door; take the time to mean it, and put a little passion in your kisses. Take delight in your spouse and in your love for each other, as Solomon and his bride did: "Let him kiss me with the kisses of his mouth: for thy love is better than wine" (Song of Sol. 1:2). Do you feel the same way about your spouse? If not, make showing your love (love deposits) a priority. I guarantee that if you continue making love deposits, you will reap a heavenly return in your marriage.

Excuses Are Not Acceptable

The third area of my marriage in which the Lord awoke me concerned my disrespect for Lewis. I did not show disrespect intentionally. I didn't realize that I was not honoring my man of God as I should have. Even though Lewis wasn't doing what he should have been doing spiritually, according to my standards, this gave me no excuse to look at him as anything other than the head of our marriage and family. Because I was the one who was growing spiritually, it was even more my responsibility to submit to the Word of God by submitting to my husband. Still, I questioned how he could lead me, especially in the things of God, if he wasn't even going to church.

Lewis was a born-again believer when we met and was very involved in church, but when his mom passed away, he became angry with God. Sadly, my failure to submit didn't bring him any closer to the Lord. He couldn't see God's love in anything, and even though I was going to church, my witness was hypocritical. Instead of loving him and showing him compassion and tenderness, I condemned him for not being where I was, for not being where he should be, and for not being a godly father in raising our girls.

The Lord finally told me to leave Lewis alone and concentrate on God. So I kept my mouth shut, continued doing things in the church, enrolled in ministerial school, and did everything else God told me to do. It has now been several years since we reconciled, and things are so much better. However, it took years to start seeing the fruit of my labor.

I knew change was coming when Lewis came downstairs one night when I was reading the Bible and asked, "Baby, can we do Bible study together?"

I said, "Yes, why?"

He said, "I want what you have—the Word of God in me."

Hallelujah! As I stated before, Lewis is now hungry for the Lord. He is reading the Word. We pray together more, and he goes to church much more. Look how God can move on your behalf when you make a decision to change. The Bible is true, and the truth will set you free. Lewis has been won over by my behavior. How? Because I let "no corrupt communication proceed out of [my] mouth, but that which is good to the use of edifying, that it may minister grace" unto Lewis (Eph. 4:29). All God wants us to do is lead by example—show people his love in our lives so they can be won over. So we need to stop looking at people, especially our spouses, through our own eyes and start seeing them as God sees them.

Both forgiveness and love are dependent not upon your feelings but on an act of your will as you respond to God working through you. For example, your spouse may do something that is disrespectful to you. You have told them over and over again to stop, but they continue. Their excuse is, "This is how I am." Although excuses are not acceptable and all who love Christ should be willing to change, do you walk around mad, with unforgiveness in your heart? No, you reach deep down within to forgive and to love them in spite of what they say. This allows God in you to be shown through your walking in forgiveness and love because you are trying to reach the place where he becomes greater than you are. When I know that by myself I wouldn't be able to respond in love in certain situations, I know that God is operating in my life because I am able to do so anyway.

I believe that when I wasn't doing what I should have been doing, I stopped Lewis's spiritual growth. My witness of Christ was simply ugly. It had no love in it. My nagging, complaining, yelling, condemning, and talking back, then crying before the Lord, "Lord, I honor you," was hypocritical, because we can't honor God when we don't honor the spouse he has given us. Most importantly, the responsibility for doing the right thing lies with the individual who is strongest in Christ. In my marriage, that was me. My responsibility was to continue developing my relationship with God. As I grew in the Lord by obeying his Word and letting him work with Lewis, Lewis's relationship with God grew.

You cannot judge others by your standards, perspectives, and experiences or else you will be judged by the very same standards. We are quick to look at and judge others without considering the sin in our own lives. You are not responsible for changing others. You are only responsible for examining and changing yourself (see 1 Cor. 11:28).

And men, your wife's failure to submit is not an excuse for you to disobey God. As the head of the household, you need to continue to lead by example and pray for her. The Bible says we can have whatever we ask for (see Mark 11:24). Therefore, pray for what you want in your spouse in accordance with the Word of God. Although Lewis wasn't what I wanted him to be, every time someone at church asked about him, I would say, "He's fine. He is a man after God's own heart. He will do great works and help finance the growth of our church." Guess what? I now have what I said.

What if you are married to a foolish person, as Abigail was in 1 Samuel 25? Her husband, Nabal, was a rich man, but he was "evil in his doings," stubborn and ill-mannered (v. 3). The Bible says Abigail was a woman of "good understanding" and "beautiful" (v. 3). Abigail was a wise woman. David and his men protected Nabal's flocks and shepherds, but when David asked him for help, Nabal refused and pretty much told them where to go. David was furious and decided to kill Nabal and his men. When Abigail was told that David was sending men to harm them and why, she immediately prepared a feast for David, treating him with the respect he deserved. She intervened for her husband. She knew the Word of God and told David that if he would not take revenge, God would reward him and take care of him. And that's just what happened.

This story is important for both men and women. Just because your spouse may act foolishly, that doesn't mean that you should as well. Humble yourself before God and before your spouse. Use the wisdom God has given you. Pray that your spouse may have the wisdom of God if he or she is not yet who God would have him or her to be.

Unforgiveness

After Lewis and I separated and sought counseling, a grudge came out. For two years, Lewis had held on to something I had no idea was affecting him. I had no idea that he had unforgiveness in his heart toward me. When he told me about it, I responded by letting him know that he should have known my heart and that I would never do anything intentionally to hurt him or one of his family members. At that moment, I felt as if something was released in our relationship. It was as if that apology was a bulldozer that tore down walls, and we were able to start rebuilding.

You cannot build or rebuild your relationship with unforgiveness in your heart. If you are the one dealing with unforgiveness, you need to confront the other person. The majority of the time, that person does not even know they have offended you. Even if you think they know or should know about the offense, it is still your responsibility to go to them and let them know how you feel (see Matt. 5:23–24). Conversely, if someone comes to you and apologizes for an offense, you must forgive them.

> **forgive:** to excuse an offense or to pardon.
> This means completely releasing your right to be
> angry or hurt. Forgiveness is not always a one-
> time event; sometimes it is a continual process.

Get rid of the cliché, "I'll forgive, but I won't forget." I thank God, because his love forgives and forgets. Isaiah 43:25 says that God blots out our sins completely and will not remember them again. Praise God! Therefore, we too must forgive, though it may not be possible to forget. However, forgiveness can still be a decision, in that when the incident comes to mind, you refuse to give that thought power by choosing not to bring it up or use it against the person.

I heard a preacher on television say that as long as you have relationships, you will get hurt. And people only hurt you because you let them in your heart. But we are all humans, and we make mistakes. I know I have hurt people that I never thought I would, but it has taught me two things: (1) I am actually human and can fall short sometimes, and (2) I have not reached the point of spiritual maturity. I know that I am constantly being tested by God because he is teaching me about character. To pass the test, I must say I'm sorry and change that behavior or forgive the person who offended me. "And even if he sins against you seven times in a day, and turns to you seven times and says, I repent [I am sorry], you must forgive him (give up resentment and consider the offense as recalled and annulled)" (Luke 17:4 AMP).

> **sin:** missing the mark of God's will by choice and because of human weakness; any action or attitude that disobeys God, betrays him, or fails to do good

It's extremely difficult for us to receive apologies from someone who does something over and over again, but we all fall short constantly, and God forgives us over and over again. No one is higher than God, and if God freely forgives you for your wrongdoings, surely you can forgive others for theirs (see Mark 11:25).

When we repent of our sins, forgiveness should follow. Therefore, forgiveness is a "must" to maturing in your Christian walk. If you understand God's forgiveness of your sins (which you commit daily), then you should immediately grant the same forgiveness to someone who apologizes to you. Only through God's love and compassion in you can you totally release forgiveness to others. How many times are you supposed to forgive? Jesus says seventy times seven (see Matt. 18:21–22). So guess what? If your spouse does the same thing over and over again, what are you supposed to do? Forgive!

In extreme cases, such as adultery or physical abuse, you still must forgive the other person even if it is in your best interest to get out of the marriage. Forgiving someone does *not* mean that you have to become their victim if they are doing things that are inappropriate. But if you keep telling your husband to put the toilet seat down, don't get mad when he forgets. Or if you continue to tell your wife to stop spending money and she doesn't, still forgive.

You must understand God's forgiveness in order to grant forgiveness to others:

- The nature of God is to forgive sins (see Neh. 9:17).
- When God forgives you, he forgives completely (see Heb. 8:12).
- God's forgiveness costs you nothing, but it was very costly to God (see John 3:16).
- God never withholds forgiveness when sins (no matter what they are) are confessed (see 1 John 1:9).

Therefore, you are to forgive others just as God has forgiven you. You are to

- willingly grant forgiveness whenever another confesses sin to you;
- forgive any type of sin, no matter how severe or devastating it might seem;
- forgive completely and not remind the forgiven person of their sin;
- forgive others in your heart and mind before they ask—or even if they *don't* ask for forgiveness.

Forgiveness is an act of obedience to God's Word and an act of kindness toward the person you're forgiving. Regardless of who is at fault, it is the responsibility of an obedient believer to begin the process of reconciliation through forgiveness. God tells us that obedience is better than sacrifice (see Matt. 9:13; 12:7). Therefore, in your love for God and your obedience to his Word, you can forgive.

You Reap What You Sow

Love is not just a feeling. It is a deep, enduring concern for another's welfare. Have you ever wondered why marriage is hard for some and not for others? Maybe it is because some went into it with a heart to give and please, while others went into it with selfish and ungodly motives (for example, money, fame, loneliness, or running away from something). Marriage, contrary to popular opinion, is not give and take. It is not 50–50. It is all about giving! I know this sounds crazy; however, everything we do, we should do it unto God. We must believe that if we do what is right, God will reward us. Trust me, I was getting tired of giving. But I was always reminded of the Scripture that says, "And let us not be weary in well doing: for in due season we shall reap, if we faint not" (Gal. 6:9). If you give, give, and give, then after a while, the other person is going to want to bless you, so they will give, give, and give in return. If both are giving, then both are happy. Luke 6:37–38 says,

> Don't pick on people, jump on their failures, criticize their faults—unless, of course, you want the same treatment. Don't condemn those who are down; that hardness can boomerang. Be easy on people; you'll find life a lot easier. Give away your life; you'll find life given back, but not merely given back—given back with bonus and blessing. Giving, not getting, is the way. Generosity begets generosity.
>
> Message

This sums up all I have been saying about sowing and reaping in your relationship with your spouse and others. As the Scripture points out, what you sow negatively will also come back around to hurt you. Therefore, if you are one who criticizes, is full of anger, displays hatred, or lies, it will boomerang. If you sow blessings to those who you think may not even deserve it, the blessings will be given to you in a greater measure. In Galatians 6:7, Paul echoes this truth: "Be not deceived; God is not mocked: for whatsoever a man soweth that [and that only] he also will reap." You have to sow love, repentance, change, forgiveness, peace, and patience in your marriage to reap the same benefits. What are you reaping from your marriage? If you don't like what you are reaping, look at what you are sowing and change your behavior. In other words, repent!

---

repent: to acknowledge wrongdoing and make a commitment to change. When we repent, not only do we change inwardly but also we change outwardly. These changes are visible to those around us.

True repentance (changed ways of thinking resulting in changed behavior) results in a changed life with new or different behavior that makes your repentance real and visible. For example, if you find yourself nagging your spouse (such as about hanging up their clothes, their whereabouts, or going to church) and God reveals for you to stop, your repentance should be visible to your spouse. If you truly repent, your spouse should notice that you do not nag him or her about those issues anymore. Someone has to start the process of repentance. Why not you?

If you are in an adulterous affair, *get out*! Adultery is an act of disobedience to God. Therefore, when you are in an adulterous affair, you are sinning not only against your spouse but against God (see Gen. 39:9). You also are destroying your own soul (see Prov. 6:32). But even if you do end the affair, don't expect to experience no consequences of your actions. Although God forgave David when he committed adultery, David still had to suffer the consequences of his sin.

The enemy works extremely hard in this area, and we need to develop the character trait of self-control. Therefore, we must put appropriate boundaries around the male/female relationships outside of our marriages. If you have already gone through the devastation of a spouse having an affair, please consider receiving counseling through your church or elsewhere to help you both work through any unresolved issues resulting from the affair.

Repent Biblically

We should *repent biblically* for a couple of reasons. Matthew 3:8 says, "Bring forth fruit that is consistent with repentance [let your lives prove your change of heart]" (AMP). Luke 3:8 states, "Bear fruits that are deserving and consistent with [your] repentance [that is, conduct worthy of a heart changed, a heart abhorring sin]. And do not begin to say to yourselves, We have Abraham as our father; for I tell you God is able from these stones to raise up descendants for Abraham" (AMP). (Note: Continue reading Luke 3 through verse 14. It discusses the changes that the people needed to make.) Jesus is saying that you can no longer use the excuse that you are a descendant of Abraham when you have no fruit (godly characteristics or Christian character and behavior). Repentance must be seen. You should demonstrate a change in behavior and not just say, "I'm sorry, Lord," yet continue to do the same thing over and over.

Another reason we should *repent biblically* is because our change will bring others to repentance—back into a right relationship with God. Second Peter 3:9 says, "The Lord does not delay and is not tardy or slow about what He promises, according to some people's conception of slowness, but He is long-suffering (extraordinarily patient) toward you, not desiring that any should perish, but that all should turn to repentance" (AMP). God's love and promises are waiting for all who will repent.

God doesn't want one person to miss heaven. As Christians, we have a responsibility to live our lives in a way that is consistent with our faith and to help others as well. I can't tell you how many people's lives I have had a chance to impact because of my decision to change. Although this change started in my home, its impact went further. It has affected all my relationships and even how I deal with strangers. I am in no way bragging because it is a daily fight between what my flesh wants to do and what God wants me to do. Because of the lifestyle changes I made as a wife, my husband—who once was mad at God, didn't want to tithe, and didn't go to church—is now loving God, reading the Bible, tithing, and attending church regularly. God was waiting for Lewis to repent and come back to him. I believe it was God's love demonstrated through me that brought my husband to repentance. A person who *repents biblically* will not only be in a right relationship with God and others but also will win lost souls for him. Moreover, a person who *repents biblically* is a changed person.

Prayer

Lord, my prayer echoes the words of Paul in Colossians 1:9–12: For this reason, since the day you sent [your spouse's name] to me, I have not stopped praying for [your spouse's name] and our marriage and asking you to fill us with the knowledge of your will through all spiritual wisdom and understanding. And I pray this in order that [your spouse's name] and I may live a life worthy of you, Lord, and may please you in every way: bearing fruit in every good work, growing in the knowledge of God, being strengthened with all power according to your glorious might so that we may have great endurance and patience, and joyfully giving thanks to the Father, who has qualified us to share in the inheritance of the saints in the kingdom of light. Thank you, Lord, that there is no condemnation—no guilt—for those who are in Christ Jesus. Thank you that where I fall short, you are my strength. Thank you for your Son, Jesus, who died for me so that my sins are forgiven. Help me to see where I fall short of your glory. Lord, I repent of all the things I have done and said that are not of you. Wash me thoroughly from my iniquity and cleanse me from my sin, for I acknowledge my transgressions and I am sorry for my sins. Create in me a clean heart, O Lord, and renew a right spirit within me. Help me to change in the areas you are revealing to me. Keep me pure and holy and righteous before you. Give me the strength I need to live a godly life. Help me to keep my mind stayed on you. Thank you that I am already changed. In Jesus's name, amen.

For an additional marriage resource, visit www.marriage101.us for the free article "Establishing True Intimacy."

ALT**R**UISM:

Repent Biblically

> Success in marriage does not come merely through finding the right mate, but through being the right mate.
>
> Barnett Brickner

T he goal of this section is to help you *repent biblically*. In this section, ask yourself how your wrong attitudes or sinful behaviors affect your loved ones. Does or can the pleasure of your sin hurt your spouse in any way? The answer is yes. Does it hurt God? The answer is unequivocally yes. Therefore, the goal of this chapter is to give you the desire to repent, renew your mind, and make a commitment to trust God by listening to and obeying what he reveals to you concerning the changes you need to make. A person who changes his or her attitude and behavior is someone who has *repented biblically*. Therefore, bring forth fruit (character) that is consistent with your repentance. Let your life prove your change of heart.

Biblical Example: Hosea and Gomer (Book of Hosea)

The book of Hosea illustrates God's faithfulness to a sinful people. Marriage is ordained by God and is symbolic of our relationship with him. God used Hosea's life to show the Israelites (as well as us today) how they were committing spiritual adultery. God told Hosea to marry a woman, Gomer, who would not remain faithful to him and would bear children by other men during their marriage. Hosea was obedient and married her. She committed adultery and decided to leave Hosea to continue that inappropriate lifestyle. However, Hosea remained faithful and did what God told him to do concerning his adulterous wife. If anyone had a right to divorce, it was Hosea—but he didn't divorce her. He actually loved her as God intended because God wanted to give people a living example of unconditional love, faithfulness, and forgiveness. Even when we are unfaithful to God—not living our lives according to our faith in God's Word—he still loves us and is willing to forgive us once we repent and turn back to him. Hosea's loyalty to his wife is a reflection of God's love and faithfulness to us.

Scripture Meditation

Meditate on the following Scriptures, which show you how to *repent biblically*. Ask God to show you areas—including all of the secret ones—in which you need to repent and change. Write down anything God reveals to you in the space after each verse.

Matthew 3:2 (AMP)

"Repent (think differently; change your mind, regretting your sins and changing your conduct), for the kingdom of heaven is at hand."

_____

_____

_____

_____

_____

Mark 11:25

"And when ye stand praying, forgive, if ye have ought against any: that your Father also which is in heaven may forgive you your trespasses."

Luke 17:3–4 (AMP)

"Pay attention and always be on your guard [looking out for one another]. If your brother sins (misses the mark), solemnly tell him so and reprove him, and if he repents (feels sorry for having sinned), forgive him. And even if he sins against you seven times in a day, and turns to you seven times and says, I repent [I am sorry], you must forgive him (give up resentment and consider the offense as recalled and annulled)."

---

1 John 1:9

"If we confess our sins, he is faithful and just to forgive us our sins, and to cleanse us from all unrighteousness."

Isaiah 1:16–20 (NLT)

"Wash yourselves and be clean! Let me no longer see your evil deeds. Give up your wicked ways. Learn to do good. Seek justice. Help the oppressed. Defend the orphan. Fight for the rights of widows. 'Come now, let us argue this out,' says the LORD. 'No matter how deep the stain of your sins, I can remove it. I can make you as clean as freshly fallen snow. Even if you are stained as red as crimson, I can make you as white as wool. If you will only obey me and let me help you, then you will have plenty to eat. But if you keep turning away and refusing to listen, you will be destroyed by your enemies. I, the LORD, have spoken!'"

_____

_____

_____

_____

_____

Self-Examination

1. What have I done and/or what can I do to rekindle our love affair? Was there a problem or incident that caused our marriage to change for the worse? If so, how can I help to resolve it?

2. Are there things I have done or said to my spouse for which I need to repent? (*If yes, list those things, confess them, and pray that God would reveal to you how to correct them.*)

3. Are there things my spouse has done that I need to forgive? (*If yes, list those things, and then release them to God and forgive your spouse. You can go one step further and talk with your spouse about it and let him or her know that you have forgiven the offense and released it to God once and for all.*)

4. If my spouse (or potential mate) could change anything about me, what would it be? Will that change stop arguments and bring peace back into our relationship and home? If yes, what would it take for me to repent and change that particular behavior?

5. Am I in right standing with God? Do I acknowledge him in the morning and throughout the day? Do I need to pray more? (*If you are not sure where you stand with God, then you can start again right now.*)

Developing Character

Make a list of changes God has revealed to you that you need to make in your relationship. Repent of all your wrongdoings and start working on each one.

Affirmation

I will keep your Word in my heart that I may not sin against you.

Reflections

_____

_____

_____

_____

_____

_____

_____

_____

_____

_____

_____

_____

_____

_____

_____

_____

_____

_____

_____

_____

_____

_____

7

The Awakening

True Love Awaits

And this is life eternal, that they might know thee the only true God, and Jesus Christ, whom thou hast sent.

John 17:3

We walk in darkness until we accept Jesus as our Lord and Savior. Christ is the way, the truth, and the light. He is our Prince Charming. Just as Prince Charming kissed Sleeping Beauty and she awoke with a smile on her face and love in her heart, when we give our lives to Christ, love takes on a whole new meaning. By developing a relationship with him, we become like him, which is love.

Christ, the Foundation

Now that you have accepted Jesus as your Lord, you are married to Christ. And because of that covenant, you have a responsibility to seek his ways and adhere to his commandments. Because of his love for you and me, we have more than eternal life in heaven. We have heaven here on earth, with him on the inside of us, guiding and directing our paths. How do you know if he is in you and you are in him? "But whoever keeps His word, truly the love of God is perfected in him. By this we know that we are in him" (1 John 2:5 NKJV). This perfected love—God's love—is what we call *agape* love.

> **agape:** an unconditional love; the Greek word for selfless love, the type of love that characterizes God. Agape is primarily an act of the will rather than emotion. This love is the greatest and most enduring of all Christian virtues.

Love gives, and God's type of love (agape love) will allow you to have the type of marriage you desire, but it involves sacrifice. The love seen in the Scriptures demonstrates a sacrificial act for another. Because of God's unconditional love for us, he gave us his only begotten Son. Jesus's unconditional love for you and me was manifest when he laid down his life so that we could be reconciled to God to have eternal life. This type of agape love is handed down to you and me, and it allows us to extend that same unconditional love to others, especially our spouses.

Let me prepare you: when you make a decision to extend unconditional love, you will find all kinds of challenges are going to come up to try to deter you from loving the way God has commanded. Your mind is going to tell you, "That person doesn't deserve it!" You'll begin to relive past hurts caused by that person. You'll want to protect yourself from getting hurt again. Don't be discouraged! Don't allow the enemy to rob you of what you will discover on the other side of your obedience to God, which is a happy, loving, and fulfilling marriage. Extending unconditional love to your spouse is an act of your will not based on how you feel. It is a completely

selfless act. Even if your spouse does not love you in the same manner or demonstrate the behavior you desire, you are still obligated
to love the way God has commanded. This was hard for me at first
because I kept saying, "How can I love this man unconditionally,
Lord, when he has done and continues to do so many things that
(I think) are wrong?" When I first learned the meaning of agape
love, it was definitely a challenge. However, even with my initial
hesitation, I was determined to love like God. I knew deep down
inside that it was the right thing to do. I also knew that God was
showing me how to have the successful marriage I so desperately
desired. His guidance in helping me to have a great marriage had
me doing things I wouldn't normally do. For example, apologizing when I knew I was right or fixing Lewis dinner right after an
argument. I learned that unconditional love went so beyond who
I was, but when I did it, I was becoming like God. Of course, on
several occasions I fell short of extending unconditional love to my
husband, as you may also. However, when you fall short, don't be
discouraged. Repent and pick up where you left off in your decision
to demonstrate agape love.

If you are spending any time building a relationship with God
through prayer or reading the Bible, he will show you when you have
missed the mark of his best for your life. He will speak to you in a
soft voice right in the middle of a situation and tell you what you
should have done that would have pleased him or what you should
do to make it right. When that happens, simply listen to the voice
of God and do what he is instructing you to do. It will be difficult at
first to do the opposite of what you were thinking of doing or saying
right in the middle of a situation. But as you continue practicing
your obedience to God, doing the right thing in your relationship
with your spouse becomes easier and easier, even when your feelings are telling you to do otherwise.

To practice biblical love for others requires you to do things you
do not want to do. Biblical love is not based on your feelings or your

plans. For example, say you are getting ready to have a big night out. You need to run some errands to prepare for the evening (get your hair and nails done, go to the store, go to the cleaners, etc.). Your spouse asks you to clean the house because it's messy. That was not in your plans, so you tell him no, and now you two are arguing. Your spouse leaves, and before you go out to start your day, you pray. God tells you to clean the house first and then run your errands. What do you do? I hope you said, "Clean the house and then run my errands." Jesus says, "My mother and my brethren are these which hear the word of God, and do it" (Luke 8:21). Remember, most of the time, God will tell you to take care of someone else's needs before your own. Of course, if you fall short, as I have, just start again the next day.

Not until you walk in agape love do you truly experience God's wonderful light (1 John 2:9). When you love the way God has commanded, his light and love will be seen and experienced by others. God is looking for those who are like him, that he may do marvelous things through them. Likewise, as a parent you expect your child to exemplify the behaviors you've taught them. God is love and so are his children. Are you a child of God? Do you exemplify his character? This is a question we should get into the habit of asking ourselves daily.

According to the Bible, God's plan for marriage is for one man and one woman to marry for a lifetime. Both the husband and wife must have a mutually supportive attitude if they are to succeed in building a harmonious home.

> For we are fellow workmen (joint promoters, laborers together) with and for God; you are God's garden and vineyard and field under cultivation, [you are] God's building. According to the grace (the special endowment for my task) of God bestowed on me, like a skillful architect and master builder I laid [the] foundation, and now another [man] is building upon it. But let each [man] be careful how he builds upon it, for no other foundation can anyone lay than that which is [already] laid, which is Jesus Christ (the Messiah, the

Anointed One). But if anyone builds upon the Foundation, whether it be with gold, silver, precious stones, wood, hay, straw, the work of each [one] will become [plainly, openly] known (shown for what it is); for the day [of Christ] will disclose and declare it, because it will be revealed with fire, and the fire will test and critically appraise the character and worth of the work each person has done. If the work which any person has built on this Foundation [any product of his efforts whatever] survives [this test], he will get his reward. But if any person's work is burned up [under the test], he will suffer the loss [of it all, losing his reward], though he himself will be saved, but only as [one who has passed] through fire.

1 Corinthians 3:9–15 AMP

If you build your home on any foundation other than Christ, the house will fall when the storms come. This is why there are so many divorces, even within the church. Lewis and I are an example of this problem—even though we were both saved, our marriage was not built on the Word of God. Our marriage was almost destroyed because we didn't understand the true meaning of agape love. Learning how to love people unconditionally, especially your spouse, requires a willingness to tap into something greater than yourself (as 1 John 4:4 says, greater is he that is on the inside of you). Most of us are trying to fix our marriages without God. We don't really know what the Bible says about how we should treat one another. His way is perfect, and his foundation is sure and strong. To build strong, godly marriages, we must build them upon a strong foundation.

So what do you do when you realize that your marriage was not built on a strong foundation? Reestablish the house (your family) on the strong foundation of Christ, which means reading the Word and doing all that it tells you to do. Laying your new foundation requires one brick at a time. For example, making a decision to not cuss at your spouse one day is a start. As Proverbs says, "Through skillful and godly Wisdom is a house (a life, a home, a family) built, and by understanding it is established [on a sound and good foundation], and by knowledge shall its chambers [of every area] be filled with all precious and pleasant riches" (Prov. 24:3–4 AMP).

Why are people divorcing? God says, "My people [marriages] are destroyed for lack of knowledge" (Hosea 4:6). Building and maintaining a harmonious home involves arming yourselves with knowledge. Here are some ways to keep learning:

- Find a mentor couple who have a great marriage and have been married for a long time to help you when you have questions and/or concerns.
- Read marriage books and magazines which will help you to see that all marriages have problems and that solutions can be found in Scripture.
- Attend marriage enrichment meetings and conferences that will help you to rebuild and strengthen your marriage.
- Get involved in your church's marriage ministry.

Couples should continually seek sound biblical knowledge when it comes to marriage. These tools will help you rebuild and/or maintain a strong marital foundation.

Religion Versus Relationship

It is important that we move away from religion, in the sense of a distant, systematic reverence for God, to a relationship that is personal and intimate with him. When I was growing up, all I knew about having a relationship with God was going to church every Sunday. Reading the Bible, praying, and entering into God's presence in my home was not a reality. I thought that I had only one day a year, my birthday, to ask God for something I really wanted. Sometimes I didn't even feel worthy to ask, but now I know and have experienced for myself a loving, gracious, and giving God who loves me in spite of my faults and sins. He is longing for me—and all of us—to talk with him and spend time with him every day. Going to church is not enough. Going to Bible study is not enough. Even these things can be a form of empty religion, because if we never really experience God in an intimate way, we don't have a relationship with him. To build a successful marriage, you have to build a personal relationship with God in order to know and hear his voice to provide you instruction.

When Lewis and I separated, my first thought was that I needed to call the church for counseling, and I did. Lewis and I actually started counseling sessions. But I realized that I have an intimate relationship with God, and I thought, *There is only one person who knows all and can tell me exactly what I need to do. That is God.* Marriage counseling and even marriage coaching can be very beneficial, but at that time what I needed was to reconnect with God so he could transform my heart. So I began to seek his face. I entered into his presence with praise and worship. I got into a quiet place where I asked questions and opened my ears to hear from him. I read the Bible more, and I let it convict my heart. Then I began to change.

In our quiet time with God, we must seek his face and will for our lives. I remember the voice of God asking me three times if I loved him. I answered, "Yes, Lord, with all my heart." He said, "Then keep my commandments!" The more you read the Word, the more you experience who he is. Why? Because the Word is God (see John 1:1).

True love awaits you, and it's only through that intimate relationship that you will experience life more abundantly.

> For the [true] love of God is this: that we do His commands [keep His ordinances and are mindful of His precepts and teaching]. And these orders of His are not irksome (burdensome, oppressive, or grievous).
>
> 1 John 5:3 AMP

God yearns to develop a relationship with you. He desires to help you and give you all that your heart desires. He also wants to restore all those things that have been stolen or lost from your life—especially in your marital relationship. I believe when I finally went to him in desperation concerning my marriage, he said, "Finally, Jewell—I've been waiting to get to know you."

In 2 Chronicles 7:14 the Lord states, "If my people, which are called by my name, shall humble themselves, and pray, and seek my face, and turn from their wicked ways; then will I hear from heaven, and will forgive their sin, and will heal their land." I did just that: I humbled myself, prayed, sought his face, and turned from doing things my way, and he healed (restored) my marriage. Just remember, God can fix the problems in your marriage, but you are required to do the work. If you and your spouse are at a point where you are unable to talk through issues, or if there are any abuse issues, then you would be wise to seek help from a Christian counselor or a pastor at your church.

Disciples of Christ

It is our responsibility as Christians to become disciples of Christ. We were created in his image and likeness to not only be in fellowship with him but to be like him on the earth. When we get to that place, we can love as he loves. God has called us to be his disciples in the world, but to be his disciples, we must love people—especially our spouses—as God loves them. It is God's Word that will transform us into his marvelous light. Therefore, "Let your light so shine before men that they may see your moral excellence and your praiseworthy, noble, and good deeds and recognize and honor and praise and glorify your Father Who is in heaven" (Matt. 5:16 AMP).

disciple: a follower of Christ; one who accepts his will and his commands and assists

> in spreading his message. Discipleship requires
> discipline and love.

In Mark 16:15, Jesus told his disciples, "Go ye into all the world, and preach the gospel to every creature." Does this apply to those eleven disciples only? No. Does it pertain only to pastors? No. They couldn't possibly reach every person. When we chose to follow Christ, *we* became the disciples he continues to speak to and through today.

Christianity is not a title. Christianity is God using people on earth to be good witnesses for him. To be a Christian is to say, "I am love, and love can be seen in me and experienced through me." This walk of faith is not about you, your spouse, or even your children. It is about advancing the kingdom of God through every aspect of life. Unbelievers need to see Christ in us to want to become Christians. Is there anyone who has been influenced to serve God because of you being a good disciple?

In James 1:22–23, God says, "But be ye doers of the Word [obey the message], and not merely listeners to it, betraying yourselves [into deception by reasoning contrary to the Truth]. For if anyone only listens to the Word without obeying it *and* being a doer of it, he is like a man who looks carefully at his [own] natural face in a mirror" (AMP). When you are a hearer only, you don't change; you continue doing the same things and acting the same way. However, when you become a doer of the word, you are changed and transformed into someone new, someone who is blessed.

That is why we need to do what the Word of God tells us: because God is looking at us to see himself in us. Remember, we are made in his image and likeness. When we accept Jesus and are led by the Spirit of God, we become children of God (see Rom. 8:14). Just as we reflect the physical and emotional characteristics of our earthly parents, we now can become transformed spiritually to reflect the personality of our heavenly Father. For example, as a child I was raised by my stepfather and biological mother, so I have taken on the characteristics of my stepfather more than those of my biological father. I am not trying to take anything away from my biological father, but my stepfather has had the greater influence on me because we have spent more quality time together. On the outside, I look just like my biological father, but the inside of me has the characteristics of my stepfather. This example illustrates that although we have an earthly father, we can still develop the characteristics and personality of our heavenly Father.

To do this, we must get to know him on a very personal level by reading his Word and doing what he says. Just as God gives us new mercy every day, we have an opportunity to provide new mercy to our spouse by loving them daily, forgiving them of wrongdoing, and allowing them to be themselves. Freely as Jesus has given to you and me, freely we should give (see Matt. 10:8). Again, your spouse could be fussing and cussing all day, acting like a fool, and you might feel that he doesn't even deserve your love and not want to do a thing for him. New mercy allows you to forgive him before you go to bed and still fix him breakfast the next day. Your love should not be conditional (what the Greeks called *phileo* love). Unconditional love gives and loves in spite of how someone is or is not treating you. That's when you know you are truly being changed and loving the way God loves us.

> **phileo:** a conditional love. Represents "tender affection" toward another, which is usually based on emotions.

When you hold on to hate, anger, strife, resentment, or other feelings that do not show God's love toward another, you give the enemy an opportunity to come in your life (see Eph. 4:26–27, 31). When you continue in that behavior or focus on the problem instead of God's Word, you give the enemy full reign in your life. The enemy uses those small cracks (problems) in your marriage and widens them further until they become so overwhelming that it's hard to get back on track. For example, an argument can turn into days of not communicating (you are socially disconnected), and then you may start sleeping in separate bedrooms (you are physically disconnected). By then you are so angry (you are emotionally disconnected) that you start to have doubts about your marriage (you are mentally disconnected), and eventually, this could lead to division (separation and/or divorce). At that point you ask yourself, *How did we get here?* This is the exact sequence of events that Lewis and I experienced. As you can see, if you give the enemy an inch, he will go for it. That is why Scripture says, "When angry, do not sin; do not ever let your wrath (your exasperation, your fury or indignation) last until the sun goes down" (Eph. 4:26 AMP). Just taking that little step will save your marriage from having major troubles.

John 10:10 says of the enemy, "The thief comes only in order to steal and kill and destroy" (AMP). The devil will try to rob you of the intimacy, love, and joy you feel toward your mate. Destroy the work of the enemy with the kind of love that only comes from God. I've learned to destroy the works of the enemy through demonstrating love. When I demonstrate love, I become like God. Therefore, I will always be victorious. Furthermore, Jesus continues, "I came that they may have and enjoy life, and have it in abundance (to the full, till it overflows)" (John 10:10 AMP). When Jesus is in the midst of our marriages, they should reflect an overflow of love, joy, peace, kindness, and all that God is—which is good.

About My Father's Business

God created the institution of marriage, and he is glorified when two individuals are a witness to his love on the earth. Just as the Father, Son, and Holy Spirit are one, a trinity is established in your marriage as well: you, your spouse, and Jesus. Unfortunately, the one we often leave out of our marriages is Jesus. Before Jesus started his ministry, he was studying the Word, developing a relationship with his Father, and seeking God's plan and purpose for his life. Jesus didn't do anything that his Father didn't tell him to do, nor did he have his own agenda; he was about his Father's business. Yet we think we can get married and work out the marriage and its issues by ourselves. God says we don't have to because he is with us always. If we are truly a part of the marriage trinity, everything we do and say should be what the Father tells us.

This is not difficult if we are led by the Holy Spirit and not our flesh. God is a God of simplicity. It is very easy to copy Christ. For thirty years, Jesus developed a relationship with his Father. As a young boy, he told his parents, "How is it that you had to look for Me? Did you not see and know that it is necessary [as a duty] for Me to be in My Father's house and [occupied] about My Father's business?" (Luke 2:49 AMP). It is time for our marriages to be about our Father's business. You show God you love him by being obedient to his Word. Your love for Christ will grow as you develop agape love and compassion with an overall concern for people. Your measuring stick in determining your love for God is how much you love others. Love is demonstrated through your actions, not your feelings.

How can you love a God you can't see? By loving others. First John 4:11–12 in *The Message* states, "My dear, dear friends, if God loved us like this, we certainly ought to love each other. No one has seen God, ever. But if we love one another, God dwells deeply within us, and his love becomes complete in us—perfect love!" And 1 John 4:20–21 says, "If anyone boasts, 'I love God,' and goes right on hating his brother or sister, thinking nothing of it, he is a liar. If he won't love the person he can see, how can he love the God he can't see? The command we have from Christ is blunt: Loving God includes loving people. You've got to love both" (Message).

People will have life-changing encounters with God through those who demonstrate the love of God. Often it seems as though the only time most people experience God is through a major disaster; however, we have daily opportunities to show love to others, especially to those in our circle of influence. For example, you may know a couple that is having difficulty in their marriage. Let yours be a godly example they can follow. Most couples do not know how to have a great marriage. Minister to them first by your godly behavior toward your spouse and then by teaching them what the Word says about their situation. Spend the necessary time praying for them and with them, and fellowship with them more often.

Christian men and women of God should not be getting divorced as a means to solve their problems. Don't be mistaken: just because you are a Christian does not mean you will not have challenges in your marriage. I believe you will have challenges *because* you are a Christian, because our spiritual enemy is trying to destroy God's children. I will also state the fact that if you are doing anything that will advance the kingdom of God (i.e., walking in your calling), you will face major challenges. The question is, how are you going to overcome the conflicts and challenges you face? I cannot reiterate enough that we are to represent God on earth; we are to show that his way is perfect. Again, Christianity is not a title, a religion, or what we do. It's who we are! It is a way of life. A Christian is someone who doesn't just go to church to hear the Word but also to do what the Word says (see James 1:22). God is looking for us to fulfill his will. This Christian walk is not about you or me. It is about doing our Father's business. God wants all people on earth to be reconciled to him and out of the hands of Satan. As Christians we are to witness God's love so that lost souls can be reconciled back to him.

God is a God of purpose; therefore, your marriage has a purpose. In John 17:18, Jesus says, "As thou hast sent me into the world, even so have I also sent them into the world." Just as God sent Jesus into the world to preach the gospel, likewise God uses each of us and our marriages to preach the gospel.

Love Biblically

Why should we love the way God loves? The very first reason you should *love biblically* is to demonstrate your love for God. God says, "If ye love me, keep my commandments" (John 14:15). God has a number of commandments, of course, but the first and greatest is given in Matthew 22:37–40: "'You shall love the Lord your God with all your heart, with all your soul, and with all your mind.' This is the first and great commandment. And the second is like it: 'You shall love your neighbor as yourself.' On these two commandments hang all the Law and the Prophets" (NKJV). This simply means that all of the laws God commanded and everything that the prophets have spoken are dependent upon us keeping these two commandments: love God and love your neighbor. Who is considered a neighbor?

> **neighbor:** a fellow human being; the person God has put you in contact with at any given time. This could be someone on your block, in the grocery store, or lying beside you at night.

In order to love your neighbor, you must first love God with your whole heart, soul, and mind. Then and only then will you be able to love others as God does. Again, God desires a relationship with each of his children. If you concentrate on the vertical relationship between you and your heavenly Father, it will have a dramatic effect on your relationship with your spouse. The second reason you must *love biblically* is the commandment in John 13:34–35, in which Jesus says, "A new commandment I give unto you, That ye love one another; as I have loved you, that ye also love one another. By this shall all men know that ye are my disciples, if ye have love one to another." If you consider yourself—or even want to be—a disciple of Christ, you must become a person who loves all people unconditionally. Biblical love should be demonstrated by all Christians.

Prayer

Father, I pray that you would look upon me and my spouse and seal our marriage with your love. Thank you for giving me a revelation of your agape love. Thank you for your love that has been shed abroad in my heart. I want to be about your business, and I want to walk in the destiny you have planned for me. Lord, help me to change and grow so that I may be a true disciple. I pray, Lord Jesus, that you guide my steps and help me to increase and overflow in agape love toward my spouse, children, family, friends, coworkers, and all people. In Jesus's name I pray, amen.

For more on loving biblically, visit www.marriage101.us for a free copy of the article "Love Deposits," which will give you additional ways to show your spouse love.

aLTRUISM:
Love Biblically

And now here is my secret, a very simple secret; it is only with the heart that one can see rightly, what is essential is invisible to the eye

Antoine de Saint-Exupery

The goal of this section is to help you *love biblically*. As you proceed through these exercises, ask yourself if you have ever made a statement similar to this one: "If [your spouse's name] doesn't do [some behavior you desire], then I won't do [something your spouse wants you to do]." Or "I am always the one who [name behavior here]. I am tired of doing [name behavior here]."

First Corinthians gives us a list of ways we should love. That list is your measuring stick as to whether you are loving biblically. For example, love never dies (see 1 Cor. 13:8); therefore, you can't fall out of love. Love never takes account of wrongdoing (see 1 Cor. 13:5), so you must forgive and forget. It never fails (see 1 Cor. 13:8), so you should never want to stop doing good, regardless what someone else does or doesn't do.

Walking in love is the fruit of an intimate relationship with God. You cannot have an intimate relationship with God and *not* love people, especially your spouse. You cannot dislike (or even hate) people yet say that you love God. The purpose of this chapter is to help you develop the fruit of love, which means learning to *love biblically*, like God. God's love—an agape (unconditional) love—is the perfect love that we should all strive to extend to others.

215

Biblical Example: Jacob and Rachel (Genesis 29)

Laban had two daughters. The name of the older was Leah, and the name of the younger was Rachel. Leah was not very beautiful, but Rachel was "lovely in form, and beautiful" (Gen. 29:16 NIV). Jacob told Laban, "'I'll work for you seven years in return for your younger daughter Rachel.' . . . So Jacob served Laban seven years to get Rachel, but they seemed like only a few days to him because of his love for her" (vv. 18, 20 NIV). He was willing to do whatever it took to marry her. However, Laban deceived Jacob by giving his oldest daughter instead of Rachel. When Jacob realized this, Laban's response was, "It is not our custom here to give the younger daughter in marriage before the older one" (v. 26 NIV). But because Jacob loved Rachel so much, he worked for Laban for another seven years. Jacob worked a total of fourteen years because he loved Rachel.

The love and determination it took to capture the heart of your spouse when you were dating is the same love and determination it is going to take to keep it. Again, love doesn't fail (see 1 Cor. 13:8). It doesn't stop or cease when you get married. *We* fail when our love is expected to adhere to conditions. Our love fails when we are in love with the idea of the wedding day and not the journey of the marriage. Love is a spiritual journey in which you stay on the path God has given you, believing that it will ultimately lead you into eternity.

Song of Solomon 8:7 says, "Flood waters can't drown love, torrents of rain can't put it out. Love can't be bought, love can't be sold—it's not to be found in the marketplace" (Message). It is only found in God—because he is love. God has freely given us his love. It is unconditional. Even when we do something that is not pleasing to God, he loves us anyway. That same agape love should be freely given to our spouses. No one is perfect. However, God's love is perfect, and our marriages should reflect that perfect, unconditional love that can only come from God.

Scripture Meditation

Meditate on the following Scriptures, which will show you what agape (unconditional) love is and how to operate in that love. Let God speak to you through these Scriptures so you can develop the fruit of love in your life. Write down anything God reveals to you in the space after each verse.

1 Corinthians 13:4–8 (NIV)

"Love is patient, love is kind. It does not envy, it does not boast, it is not proud. It is not rude, it is not self-seeking, it is not easily angered, it keeps no record of wrongs. Love does not delight in evil but rejoices with the truth. It always protects, always trusts, always hopes, always perseveres. Love never fails."

_____

_____

_____

_____

Matthew 5:43–48 (Message)

"You're familiar with the old written law, 'Love your friend,' and its unwritten companion, 'Hate your enemy.' I'm challenging that. I'm telling you to love your enemies. Let them bring out the best in you, not the worst. When someone gives you a hard time, respond with the energies of prayer, for then you are working out of your true selves, your God-created selves. This is what God does. He gives his best—the sun to warm and the rain to nourish—to everyone, regardless: the good and bad, the nice and nasty. If all you do is love the lovable, do you expect a bonus? Anybody can do that. If you simply say hello to those who greet you, do you expect a medal? Any run-of-the-mill sinner does that. In a word, what I'm saying is, Grow up. You're kingdom subjects. Now live like it. Live out your

God-created identity. Live generously and graciously toward others, the way God lives towards you."

_____

_____

_____

John 13:34–35 (NIV)

"A new command I give you: Love one another. As I have loved you, so you must love one another. By this all men will know that you are my disciples, if you love one another."

_____

_____

_____

John 15:8–17

"Herein is my Father glorified, that ye bear much fruit; so shall ye be my disciples. As the Father hath loved me, so have I loved you: continue ye in my love. If ye keep my commandments, ye shall abide in my love; even as I have kept my Father's commandments, and abide in his love. These things have I spoken unto you, that my joy might remain in you, and that your joy might be full. This is my commandment, That ye love one another, as I have loved you. Greater love hath no man than this, that a man lay down his life for his friends. Ye are my friends, if ye do whatsoever I command you. Henceforth I call you not servants; for the servant knoweth not what his lord doeth: but I have called you friends; for all things that I have heard of my Father I have made known unto you. Ye have not chosen me, but I have chosen you, and ordained you, that ye should go and bring forth fruit, and that your fruit should remain: that whatsoever ye shall ask of the Father in my name, he may give it you. These things I command you, that ye love one another."

_____

_____

_____

1 John 4:7–21

"Beloved, let us love one another: for love is of God; and every one that loveth is born of God, and knoweth God. He that loveth not knoweth not God; for God is love. In this was manifested the love of God toward us, because that God sent his only begotten Son into the world, that we might live through him. Herein is love, not that we loved God, but that he loved us, and sent his Son to be the propitiation for our sins. Beloved, if God so loved us, we ought also to love one another. No man hath seen God at any time. If we love one another, God dwelleth in us, and his love is perfected in us. Hereby know we that we dwell in him, and he in us, because he hath given us of his Spirit. And we have seen and do testify that the Father sent the Son to be the Saviour of the world. Whosoever shall confess that Jesus is the Son of God, God dwelleth in him, and he in God. And we have known and believed the love that God hath to us. God is love; and he that dwelleth in love dwelleth in God, and God in him. Herein is our love made perfect, that we may have boldness in the day of judgment: because as he is, so are we in this world. There is no fear in love; but perfect love casteth out fear: because fear hath torment. He that feareth is not made perfect in love. We love him, because he first loved us. If a man say, I love God, and hateth his brother, he is a liar: for he that loveth not his brother whom he hath seen, how can he love God whom he hath not seen? And this commandment have we from him, That he who loveth God love his brother also."

_____

_____

_____

Self-Examination

 1. Do I still love my spouse? Whether yes or no, explain why.

 2. Do I spend quality time with my spouse? How does my spouse like for me to express my love?

 3. How can I show love to my family? *(For example, if you yell at your spouse or children, you could lower your voice; or you could sit down with your family for dinner.)*

 4. What are at least ten things I love about my spouse? *(Compile a list. Whenever you feel like giving up or the enemy tries to tell you that you have fallen out of love, focus on this list. The enemy will always have you focus on the negatives, but God's love will allow you to focus on the positives.)*

 5. Am I emotionally withdrawn? Have I reached a state of complacency in my marriage? Do I believe that "This is just the way it is, and there is nothing I can do to change it"? *(If yes, make a firm decision that you can have a happy and fulfilling marriage. What can you do to start the process?)*

Developing Character

For thirty days and nights, make it a priority to demonstrate love to your spouse (see the Appendix, "Love Deposits," on page 249) and pray every day concerning your marriage. Remember, everything you do is unto the Lord, not to man (Eph. 6:7); and to reap love, you have to sow love (Gal. 6:7).

Affirmation

Because God is love, I am love. Therefore, I can love my spouse unconditionally and have the type of marriage I desire and that God has planned for us.

Reflections

_____

_____

_____

_____

_____

_____

_____

_____

_____

_____

_____

_____

8

Happily Ever After

Live by Faith

But all things are from God, Who through Jesus Christ reconciled us to Himself [received us into favor, brought us into harmony with Himself] and gave to us the ministry of reconciliation [that by word and deed we might aim to bring others into harmony with Him].

2 Corinthians 5:18 AMP

The story of Sleeping Beauty says she and her prince lived happily ever. As Christians, we know that we are guaranteed a "happily ever after" ending because we are promised eternal life. This walk with God is all about glorifying him and bringing others to Christ. Although we will not be married in the resurrection, God wants us to live a happy, peaceful, and prosperous life in our marriage covenant right now.

Witnessing to Others

The story of Queen Vashti's refusal to come at the king's command and the king's hasty decision to divorce her has a lot to teach us. Remember, he was angry when he asked his counselors what to do. He later realized that he had made a terrible mistake. He hadn't thought it through himself, and the men he turned to gave him self-serving advice. So here's a lesson for us: first take your problem to God, and then choose wisely the people you'll talk to because not everyone will give you good, godly advice. In the king's case, after he sobered up, he missed his wife. His counselors' advice took both the king and Vashti out of their destiny, and they sinned against God because they divorced. But God is good! He used that mistake for his glory by using Queen Esther to help the Jews.

Christians and non-Christians are all looking at our marriages to see how we are living. To the world, we are a live commercial for Jesus. When Lewis and I separated, I realized that I was a bad witness for Christ. Others would have described me as a woman of faith. However, my failing marriage was a poor testimony to believers and nonbelievers of God and his Word. Our separation made a mockery of his Word, and my behavior witnessed to others that his Word is not true. If we would have divorced, we would have told people that the Word doesn't work. After Lewis moved out, my brother, who knows who I am in Christ, told me he had thought that if any marriage would have succeeded, it would have been mine. He hoped my marriage was the one that would break the generational curse of divorce in our family. However, at that time I simply did not know how to get victory over the challenges I was facing. But I made a decision that divorce was not the answer. Working through the challenges to get to the other side took a lot of faith, patience, and work. However, when I tried to do it in my own strength, I failed; when I judged what Lewis was or wasn't doing, I failed; and when I did the opposite of what God's Word said, I failed. Those moments of disobedience always resulted in an argument or strife in our relationship. What I've learned is that our strength and ability to overcome the challenges we face rest in God's Word and applying that Word to our life.

Second Corinthians 3:3–5 says we are living letters for Christ:

> You show and make obvious that you are a letter from Christ delivered by us, not written with ink but with [the] Spirit of [the] living God, not on tablets of stone but on tablets of human hearts. Such is the reliance and confidence that we have through Christ toward and with reference to God. Not that we are fit (qualified and sufficient in ability) of ourselves to form personal judgments or to claim or count anything as coming from us, but our power and ability and sufficiency are from God.
>
> AMP

Again, our marriages are looked on as examples by those outside in the world. Our marriages are a witness—not in what we say but in what we do and how we minister to other people. Our marriages are supposed to be a window into God's unconditional love. No matter where you go, if people see God through you, they will run after God and seek you out for encouragement and spiritual advice. As Christians, we are to lead people to Christ or help those who have gone astray to get back to him.

How can we, as Christians, truly win souls for Christ if we continue to do the same things as those who don't know him? When my brother told me of his disappointment, I was hurt and sad because I knew that ultimately, I was not a good witness for Christ. God was not being glorified in my life, and I was just like others who didn't know him. As Christians, we are not supposed to be like others in the world; we are supposed to be like Christ, and people should see that difference. Why would my brother, who is separated from his wife, want to reconcile if I couldn't keep my own marriage together? Although God always loves us, he is not pleased when we don't fulfill our promise to him (our wedding vows) and when we are bad witnesses. Again, why would anyone want to give their life to Christ if Christians are just like the rest of the world? I was so ashamed, and more so because my brother was not the only one watching. My separation stopped or slowed many family members and friends from accepting Jesus as Lord of their lives.

So why don't our lives reflect the truth of God's Word? It's not that the Bible isn't true; it is because we are not implementing and living the Word of Truth. By the grace of God, Lewis and I are back together, and we are a living testimony (epistle) that God's Word works if you do what it says.

Reconciliation

If your marriage is going through a rough time, you are not in harmony with your mate. You may feel like you are going in opposite directions or not able to agree about anything.

Just as you can be reconciled to God (because Christ died for you), you can be reconciled to your spouse, but you must incorporate the things discussed in this book and do what God has revealed to you concerning your marriage.

> **reconciliation:** the process of bringing opposing parties or people together, which often requires sacrifice on both sides

Here is an example of reconciliation: at the end of the month, you compare your bank statement to your check register. If they are not in agreement, you notify the bank or make the necessary changes to correct the problem. In marriage, when you and your spouse are out of harmony, think of the Word of God as the bank statement you refer to during trials and tribulations. God's Word will reconcile you to your spouse. Find out what the Word says regarding the issue you are struggling with and make the necessary adjustments. In order for us to have better marriages, we have to do something different.

Divorce is not supposed to be an option for us as Christians. However, the Word of God makes two allowances for divorce: adultery (Matt. 5:32) and when a nonbeliever wants out (1 Cor. 7:15). If you are in an abusive situation, you may separate until your spouse gets help. In relationships where there is infidelity, abuse of any kind, or addiction, seek counseling and put accountability measures into place with trustworthy family or friends until your spouse has proven that some transformation from the old behavior has taken place. Even in serious situations like these and others, hear from God concerning your situation, and do what he tells you to do. Know that God can still heal and reconcile your marriage if you allow his grace to come into your relationship. After all, the prophet Hosea married a prostitute (see the book of Hosea). While married, she continued in that line of work and had two children who were possibly fathered by other men. However, Hosea continued to do what God had called him to do, and he and his wife reconciled. God is in the business of working miracles. He can even work things out in what appears to be an impossible situation. Just remember what Luke 1:37 says: "For with God nothing shall be impossible." Again, God's plan for marriage is different for each and every couple—seek him concerning yours.

Husbands must understand the role and the responsibility they have toward God's daughters. God says in his Word, "Husbands, in the same way be considerate as you live with your wives, and treat them with respect as the weaker partner and as heirs with you of the gracious gift of life, so that nothing will hinder your prayers" (1 Peter 3:7 NIV). This Scripture cannot be overlooked. Can you imagine needing something from the Lord and not being able to go to him in prayer because you haven't been treating your wife right? I am not just talking about violence. How do you talk to your wife? Do you treat her as the King's daughter that she is? If not, find a mature Christian male role model to help you.

Just like you, I was in a place where divorce seemed like the only option. In hindsight I realize that the challenges we were having were so minimal, even though at the time they seemed monumental. But now I am so thankful I didn't move forward with divorce. The following Scripture helped me to put it all in perspective: "For I consider that the sufferings of this present time (this present life) are not worth being compared with the glory that is about to be revealed to us and in us and for us and conferred on us!" (Rom. 8:18 AMP). That Scripture has proved so true, because Lewis and I are in a much better place than we were before.

Faith

I was taught that faith is laying hold of the unrealities of hope and bringing them into the realm of reality by acting on the Word of God. Faith can be seen when a dream finally becomes a reality, when a thought is manifested, or when you speak a thing and it comes into existence. I wanted so much to have a great marriage and to stay with my husband "until death do us part." My faith was evident when my husband and I got back together. Faith is actively doing what the Word of God says until you see the desired change. The Bible says that God's Word will not return to him void (see Isa. 55:11). If you obey God and change in the areas of your life where he is instructing you to change, in the end, your faith will be seen— not just by you but also by others.

Because I believed so strongly in God's Word, I had to find answers concerning my marriage or else my faith in him was in vain. Now I can profess (or proclaim) that God's Word is true. We can have successful, fulfilling marriages if we live by faith. We must do what the Word says, for as Scripture says, faith without works is dead (see James 2:17). I fought (and continue to fight) to have a great relationship with my husband. If we can grab hold of the fact that our love for Christ will be demonstrated through how we treat and love our spouses, then our marriages will reflect his love, and the world will see our faith.

First Timothy 6:12 tells us, "Fight the good fight of faith, lay hold on eternal life, whereunto thou art also called, and hast professed a good profession [confession of faith] before many witnesses."

> **faith:** trust and belief that what God says is true, whether he says it in his Word or in what the Holy Spirit speaks to our hearts. This trust leads us to obedience.

I am a person who loves God with all my heart and soul. Anyone who knows me, knows my faith. When Lewis and I separated, I kept hearing God say to me, "Do you love me?" I replied, "Yes, Lord, I love you." He said, "Keep my commandments."

It is impossible for most people to see a "happily ever after" when they are going through a rough time in their marriage. I know that I couldn't see that far into the future. But even when there seems to be no hope, faith allows you to get a glimpse into what is possible with God. Faith believes that if I just trust God and obey his Word, no matter what situation I am going through, God will get me through (see Prov. 3:5–6). How do you activate and develop your faith? By reading and studying the Bible and spending time with God in prayer. Faith comes by hearing, and hearing comes by the Word of God (see Rom. 10:17). Just like most people who are ready to quit, I couldn't see the good in my marriage or why I should even stay, but faith told me to keep going. And because of my faith, I was reconciled to my husband. It took work—lots of work. But I opened my ears, my mind, and my heart and allowed God to reveal himself to me and through me. Everything God told me to do, I did, and it turned out for my good. God has a good plan for your life, and it ends with a "happily ever after" on earth and in heaven if you live by faith.

Our "happily ever after" exists in Jesus Christ and in our marriages if we allow him to be in the midst of them. My faith is the reason that Lewis and I have reconciled and are still together. We are no longer moved by trials and tests that try to tear us apart because we have learned how to walk by faith and not by sight (see 2 Cor. 5:7). We also know the purpose and will of God for our marriage. If we are faithful in just the little things (such as honoring our vows), he will use us mightily for his kingdom. If you have ever felt deep within that you were going to do great things, you can. Just allow God to be God in your life and watch him work through your marriage.

Marriage Ministry

All Christians who truly want to be used by God are called to the ministry of reconciliation—that by word and deed, we might aim to bring others into harmony with him. We are to finish the work Jesus started by helping people to see that through him they have eternal life. God needs all of his children to minister to others the good news of Jesus Christ.

> **minister:** to do anything that serves the needs of another; to carry out God's Word in the actions of your life, whether by serving as an usher at church, giving your testimony to a stranger, or making breakfast for your spouse

God has chosen to work through people. That is how we become ministers of the gospel and win souls for the kingdom. How will someone know when they have an experience with God? Since God is love, if someone experiences love from you, they've experienced God. God's Word says people will know us by our fruit (Matt. 7:20). Therefore, developing godly character (fruit) and being obedient to his Word allows people to experience God.

> **fruit:** good works that can be seen by all, produced by our Christian lives. According to Scripture, the fruit of the Spirit is love, joy, peace, long-suffering, gentleness, goodness, faith, meekness, and temperance (see Gal. 5:22–23).

It is very important to understand what ministry is and is not. It is not, as most would consider it, for pastors only. Ministry is using whatever talent, skill, or ability God has given you to help him further the kingdom. Therefore, ministry for you could be serving as a doctor, nurse, schoolteacher, secretary, government employee, volunteer, or homemaker. Whatever area of business or service God is using you in is ministry.

When Jesus was finished with his mission here on earth, he prayed to God that all would know he came to give them eternal life: "And this is eternal life: [it means] to know (to perceive, recognize, become acquainted with, and understand) You, the only true and real God, and [likewise] to know Him, Jesus [as the] Christ (the Anointed One, the Messiah), Whom You have sent" (John 17:3 AMP). We are now responsible for completing that mission that Jesus started, which is to tell the world they can have eternal life through Jesus Christ. Our godly and holy lives are ministry, and what we do and say ministers life to others.

Men, understand that your wife has a God-given assignment, whether big or small. The two of you are one. God has ordained your marriage; therefore, you are packaged together in the same calling, yet with different responsibilities.

You need to know that both husband and wife have an assignment. Your husband or wife may not be seen in the public eye; however, his or her responsibilities are just as important and play a major part in your success (see 1 Cor. 12). Neither man nor woman is superior to the other. Men and women are equal in God's eyes. Neither is independent of the other (see 1 Cor. 11:11–12). In marriage, the two of you are one and God is no respecter of persons (see Acts 10:34).

Accepting the call to be a servant of God can be very demanding, but you must learn how to balance ministry and family life. You must spend quality time with your family. God has chosen you to be a faithful steward over your family. Your spouse and children are gifts from him, and you should enjoy them. According to Proverbs 31:16 (AMP), before a woman decides to take on a new assignment/ministry she makes sure she doesn't neglect her present duties. God never intended for ministry (what he specifically calls us to do) to tear couples apart. For example, when God called me to write books, I questioned him regarding how I'd do all the other things I had to do. Of course, God started waking me up at two o'clock in the morning. Not only did writing books not take away time from my family, but despite the lack of sleep, God gave me the strength throughout the day to do what I needed to do.

Couples must make an effort to spend time together, both away from their children and with their children. You are to minister first to your own family. Too often the spouse and children are neglected because of work or other responsibilities. Do not take your spouse for granted. In our home, we have a "mommy-daddy weekend" every year and a family vacation week in the summer. The weekend doesn't have to be expensive. Even if you just go into the next city to spend the night, that money is an investment in your marriage that will be well worth it! If you don't put time, money, and energy into your relationship, you will eventually reap a dead or boring marriage. I was speaking with someone who has been married more than fifty years yet does not love her husband because, as she stated, *he* never (but in reality *they* never) invested or deposited love, time, or work into their marriage. I was very sad to hear that, because I know it is not what God intended for couples. He never intended for couples to spend fifty years together completely miserable and unfulfilled. That is bondage! Divorce is not the answer either. *Change* is the answer—a change in the way a couple thinks and their behavior. As for me and Lewis, we are committed to making daily love deposits so that we will reap a loving, harmonious relationship for years to come.

An Expected End

What does it take to have a "happily ever after" marriage? Faith, hope, and love—"but the greatest of these is love" (1 Cor. 13:13 NIV). Our faith is seen by others when we live our lives by faith. Our hope encourages others through our testimony of his goodness and grace. Our love affects others because it witnesses to them of God's unconditional love. However, work produces faith; long-suffering provokes hope; and love prompts sacrifice.

I believe there are three main reasons why our marriages are not working the way God intended them to:

1. We have false expectations, unrealistic thoughts, and preconceived ideas about marriage.
2. We do not know the reason behind this marriage covenant God created or how we should live together in it.
3. We are selfish. Each spouse is always thinking it is about "me," while the whole time it is really about glorifying the Father and demonstrating his love to the world. We should be a representation of Christ on the earth.

God has a plan and a purpose for you and your spouse. It took Lewis and me a long time to discern God's purpose for us, and if I had divorced Lewis, I would have destroyed God's plan and his call on our lives. You may say to yourself, "We are just average people who love the Lord," or "God can't use this messed-up marriage." You may not see how God can use you, but God says that he can use the foolish to put the wise to shame, the weak to put the strong to shame, and what is lowborn and insignificant to bring those in power to nothing. Why does he do that? So that we won't glorify ourselves but rather will give him the glory (see 1 Cor. 1:26–31). He is waiting for someone who loves him enough to be obedient to his Word. But as Scripture says, "Eye hath not seen, nor ear heard, neither have entered into the heart of man, the things which God hath prepared for them that love him" (1 Cor. 2:9). In other words, you have no idea the blessings that are on the other side of a messed-up marriage, but you have to get to the other side to experience them.

"For I know the thoughts that I think toward you, saith the LORD, thoughts of peace, and not of evil, to give you an expected end. Then shall ye call upon me, and ye shall go and pray unto me, and I will hearken unto you. And ye shall seek me, and find me, when ye shall search for me with all your heart" (Jer. 29:11–13). Marriages were created to endure until the end. It is easy to give up and quit. It is hard to fight the good fight of faith. I hope that after reading *Marriage 101*, you will realize that it is your faith that will lead you on the path toward "happily ever after." Lewis and I will be the first to tell the world that "we have come this far by faith" in our marriage, but the best is yet to come.

Minister Biblically

Why should we *minister biblically* to others? Again, all Christians are called to be ambassadors (or ministers) for Christ in the work of reconciliation (see 2 Cor. 5:18–20). We must be about our Father's business, which is to reconcile those who are lost, "for the god of this world has blinded the unbelievers' minds [that they should not discern the truth], preventing them from seeing the illuminating light of the Gospel of the glory of Christ (the Messiah), Who is the Image and Likeness of God" (2 Cor. 4:4 AMP). That means that we are to be fishers of men (see Mark 1:17). Those who win souls are wise (see Prov. 11:30).

In addition, to be an effective minister for the kingdom of God, you must be transformed. Allow the Holy Spirit to transform your life so that you are fit for the Master's use. It is my prayer that *Marriage 101* will assist you in your transformation process. God has called each of us to do something specific for him. Many are called, but only a few choose to say, "Yes, Lord, I give you my life. Do as you please," or as Mary stated, "Be it unto me according to thy word" (Luke 1:38). But even if you say yes, first you must develop his character (the fruit of the Spirit). The fruit is love—agape love that allows you to love all people unconditionally. Your desire should be to serve and be a blessing to others. Yes, you can feed the poor and do all these great things, but if you don't have love—God's love in you—then you are a useless nobody (see 1 Cor. 13:1–3 AMP). The second thing required is that you must know what he wants you and your spouse to do and then do it. Third, you must have great faith, which allows you to act on what you believe. "Without faith it is impossible to please God" (Heb. 11:6 NIV). Last but certainly not least, we all should long to hear from God, "Well done, thou good and faithful servant" (Matt. 25:21). Therefore, go into all the world and preach the gospel of Jesus Christ (see Matt. 29:19–20), whether that is through writing books, recording music, running your business, participating in politics, starting a nonprofit organization, helping churches with their mission, or whatever else God is calling you to do—just do it.

Prayer

Heavenly Father, I can do nothing without you, but with you I can do all things. I pray that you would open my spiritual eyes and my spiritual ears, prepare my heart, and renew a right spirit in me to hear from you daily. You have created this institution of marriage. Thank you for my man (or woman) of God. Thank you that your

Word will change me first and that your works through me may minister to my spouse and others. Lord, you are indeed God and your words are true—and you have promised me good things, so do as you have promised! Bless me and my family forever! Help us to have a happy and peaceful marriage. Help us to know and fulfill the calling on our lives. I accept the assignment you have given to us. Show us our path so we can serve others and be a blessing to them. Let our marriage be a witness of your love and a manifestation of your Word. Because you have promised it and I am willing to be obedient to your Word, may our testimony of faith and your goodness continue until you return again, for this, O Lord, is your will. In Jesus's name, amen.

For more on this subject, visit www.marriage101.us to sign up to receive a free copy of the article, "Honor the Promise."

ALTRUIS**M**:
Minister Biblically

A successful marriage requires falling in love many times, always with the same person.

Mignon McLaughlin

The goal of this section is to equip you to *minister biblically* to the people God has put in your sphere of influence. Being a minister for Jesus Christ is the responsibility of every believer, not just the clergy at your local church. You and I are ministers of the gospel as well. In our daily lives we should carry out the statutes and commandments of God. Simply put, we should live and conduct ourselves according to the Bible. Whether you know it or not, everyone around you—your family, the people at your job, the members of your church—they all are watching your life and waiting to see Jesus through you. How would others describe you? Would they say you are a good or poor witness for Christ?

We have to make a daily effort to live our lives as testimonies that Jesus Christ is alive. If we live according to God's Word, we become a witness of his love, thereby winning souls for Christ. How? Every day, people are searching for the real, authentic, true, and living God. The world will see and experience God, who dwells on the inside of us, through us. Millions of lost souls in this dark world are waiting to see the light of Jesus shine through believers like you and me. The enemy is visible and rampant today in the media, whether through TV, magazines, billboards, the news, music, or videos. Think about it. How many billboards do you see that give people a message of hope or encouragement? As Christians we are supposed to be billboards of hope, love, and encouragement in order to reconcile the world back to God. This is the ministry of reconciliation. As a couple, you also have a ministry to one another and to the people around you. God wants to use your marriage in some way, whether it is to help save just one marriage from ending in divorce or to be a witness of Christ's love to one person in your neighborhood. You and your spouse were put together by God, and you now have work to do together for him. This ministry starts at home, and once you find and submit to God's plan for your marriage, he can use you to do greater works for the kingdom. Ultimately, the goal is for you as a couple to *minister biblically* to others the Good News of Jesus Christ.

Biblical Example: Mary and Joseph (Matthew 1:18–2:23 and Luke 1:26–2:7)

This biblical example shows how God knows the purpose of every couple. This couple was engaged when God spoke to them concerning the purpose of their marriage, which was to raise a son who would fulfill God's purpose. God told them to name him Jesus and that his purpose for entering the world was to save mankind from sin. How awesome is it that God can trust parents to train and prepare a child to fulfill his or her purpose on this earth? This is why it is important to balance family and work. We have a responsibility to God and to our children to train our children to be all they can be. It is not about how big the assignment is but about your acceptance of the calling and what you do with it. When given the task, Mary accepted it willingly: "Be it unto me according to thy word" (Luke 1:38). And her faithfulness to God endured all that came with the assignment: being looked upon as an adulteress because she became pregnant with a child that was not her fiancé's; being ridiculed when she told the story of how she was a pregnant virgin; having to give birth in a barn; and seeing her son be crucified on the cross. Even in the face of uncertainty, confusion, and fear, she believed God, thereby fulfilling her assignment. Her testimony for all the world to hear is written in Luke 1:46–55.

The Bible says that Joseph was "a just man" (Matt. 1:19), which I believe means that he was a man of faith because the Bible says, "the just shall live by faith" (Gal. 3:11). I believe that Joseph prayed about his upcoming marriage to a woman who was already pregnant, and God spoke to him and told him why he should marry his future bride. Joseph could have easily gotten out of the wedding, but he knew the will of God for his life and accepted it.

God wants couples to do something for him. It could be raising a child, fulfilling an assignment, working together in ministry, or witnessing to their neighbors the love of God. Although all assignments given by God will bring struggles, challenges, and fear, the outcome not only shows your faithfulness to God but is your testimony of faith to others.

Scripture Meditation

Meditate on the following Scripture passages, which will show you how God wants to use you for the reconciliation of his people. Ask God to speak to you through these Scripture passages and to reveal your gifts and talents and how they can be used for his glory. Write down anything God reveals to you in the space after each verse.

Ephesians 4:1–2 (AMP)

"I therefore, the prisoner for the Lord, appeal to and beg you to walk (lead a life) worthy of the [divine] calling to which you have been called [with behavior that is a credit to the summons to God's service, living as becomes you] with complete lowliness of mind (humility) and meekness (unselfishness, gentleness, mildness), with

239

patience, bearing with one another and making allowances because you love one another."

_____

_____

_____

1 Peter 4:10–11

"As every man hath received the gift, even so minister the same one to another, as good stewards of the manifold grace of God. If any man speak, let him speak as the oracles of God; if any man minister, let him do it as of the ability which God giveth: that God in all things may be glorified through Jesus Christ, to whom be praise and dominion for ever and ever. Amen."

_____

_____

_____

James 2:20–24 (NIV)

"You foolish man, do you want evidence that faith without deeds is useless? Was not our ancestor Abraham considered righteous for what he did when he offered his son Isaac on the altar? You see that his faith and his actions were working together, and his faith was made complete by what he did. And the scripture was fulfilled that says, 'Abraham believed God, and it was credited to him as righteousness,' and he was called God's friend. You see that a person is justified by what he does and not by faith alone."

_____

_____

_____

2 Corinthians 5:18–20 (Message)

"All this comes from the God who settled the relationship between us and him, and then called us to settle our relationships with each other. God put the world square with himself through the Messiah, giving the world a fresh start by offering forgiveness of sins. God has given us the task of telling everyone what he is doing. We're Christ's representatives. God uses us to persuade men and women to drop their differences and enter into God's work of making things right between them. We're speaking for Christ himself now: Become friends with God; he's already a friend with you."

_____

_____

_____

2 Timothy 2:10 (AMP)

"Therefore I [am ready to] persevere and stand my ground with patience and endure everything for the sake of the elect [God's chosen], so that they too may obtain [the] salvation which is in Christ Jesus, with [the reward of] eternal glory."

_____

_____

_____

Self-Examination

1. When I said my marriage vows, who did I make those promises to? My spouse? Or to God? Will I honor those marriage vows? If so, how? Ask God to reveal the way. If not, why not?

2. What is the heart of God concerning my marriage? Do I know what the Lord has called us to do as a couple (your purpose)? *(If not, pray and seek his will. Discuss it and write down your vision/purpose together. This is separate from the vision for your family that you wrote in the Talk Biblically section.)*

3. Do I have contempt in my heart for what my spouse is called to do? If so, why? How can I seek God as to my role and help my spouse in his or her calling?

4. How can I survive the demands of juggling home life, career, and ministry responsibilities yet still enjoy having a successful and fulfilling marriage? Do I have days off? Do my spouse and I date one another? If not, establish some rules.

5. Am I a good witness or a bad witness for Christ? What can I do to win those around me for Christ?

Developing Character

You must begin to balance your time between family, work, and ministry. For this exercise, rekindle the fires that have slowly diminished in your relationship because of children, career, and other daily responsibilities. You and your spouse should plan a romantic getaway and monthly dates without the children. Use your calendars to schedule dates right now. Then, starting every January, continue scheduling time with one another for the entire year. Don't forget to schedule your daily and weekly time as well.

Affirmation

I am God's handiwork to do with as he pleases. My marriage will forever glorify him. It will be a testimony to others that God's Word is true and his way is perfect.

Reflections

_____

_____

_____

_____

_____

_____

_____

_____

_____

_____

_____

_____

_____

_____

_____

_____

_____

Conclusion

Recently I read the book *Who Moved My Cheese?* by Dr. Spencer Johnson. The concept of this book is to help readers change the way they think. Below is a particular section of the book that stood out to me because it sums up what I've been trying to get across in this book.

> A friend of mine received this revelation:
>
> I think my current relationship is "old cheese" that has some pretty serious mold on it. Or perhaps the old cheese is old behavior. What we really need to do is let go of the old behavior that is the cause of our bad relationships, then move on to a better way of thinking and acting. The New Cheese is a new relationship with the same person. I like the idea of letting go of old behavior instead of letting go of the relationship.

Repeating the same behavior will just get you the same results. Many times we think we have to start over when the answer is to change—to change our old behavior and thinking. We can have "happily ever after" if we incorporate God's way of doing things. Yes, it takes work, and it hurts sometimes because we've been trained to get rid of something or someone if it is not working. But that is not the heart of God nor the will of God for his children. We are the light in this world of darkness. We should influence nonbelievers; they should not be influencing us.

Just as with any other part of your life—career, raising children, owning a business, or having good health—you have to be diligent and consistent. You have to work at it. Marriage requires work as well, so right now, make a decision to

- renew your mind and become a doer of God's Word (act biblically);
- be led by the Holy Spirit and not your fleshly desires (identify biblically);
- speak life—the Word of God (talk biblically);
- honor God by honoring your husband or wife (submit biblically);
- become one with your spouse in spirit, soul, and body (unite biblically);
- ask God to help you change, and then *change* (repent biblically);
- establish a deeper relationship with God and your spouse (love biblically); and
- live by faith (minister biblically).

I believe that when you can read the Word, hear the Word, and understand the Word of God, then and only then can you be changed. Once you are changed, God can be glorified.

My prayer for all couples reading *Marriage 101* is taken from Ephesians 3:14–20 (NLT):

When I think of the wisdom and scope of God's plan, I fall to my knees and pray to the Father, the Creator of everything in heaven and on earth. I pray that from his glorious, unlimited resources he will give you mighty inner strength through his Holy Spirit. And I pray that Christ will be more and more at home in your hearts as you trust in him. May your roots go down deep into the soil of God's marvelous love. And may you have the power to understand, as all God's people should, how wide, how long, how high, and how deep his love really is. May you experience the love of Christ, though it is so great you will never fully understand it. Then you will be filled with the fullness of life and power that comes from God. Now glory be to God! By his mighty power at work within us, he is able to accomplish infinitely more than we would ever dare to ask or hope.

Amen.

Appendix

Love Deposits

According to Galatians 6:7, you reap what you sow. Therefore, I believe if you sow love, you will reap love. Below are thirty ways to demonstrate your love—make daily love deposits.

1. Buy your spouse a red rose.
2. Take them to lunch.
3. Kiss them passionately.
4. Tell them a funny joke.
5. Write loving messages on notecards and leave them around the house.
6. Rent a funny movie.
7. Pamper your spouse after work.
8. Buy a card.
9. Play a board game or cards.
10. Leave a message on the answering machine at work or home.

11. Let your spouse know how much you missed them while they were away.
12. Treat them to breakfast.
13. Purchase or make their favorite dessert and eat it by candlelight.
14. Watch their favorite show together.
15. Take a walk together.
16. Find a poem on the Internet or at the library—or write one—that will express your feelings and read it to them.
17. Take your family out for a treat (such as ice cream or Slurpees).
18. Pray together.
19. Make love to your spouse.
20. Give your spouse a foot massage.
21. Turn on some music and dance with your spouse.
22. Cook dinner together.
23. Speak in love all day (e.g., no nagging or negative talk).
24. Look in the local paper for an event you can do together or as a family.
25. Before bed, fix them a nighttime beverage or snack.
26. Make a decision to change one behavior your spouse does not like.
27. Hug them.
28. Start a new family tradition.
29. Let your spouse know what you love about them.
30. Schedule a family meeting just to talk.

Jewell Powell met her Prince Charming in July of 1992. Both were aware of the statistics concerning divorce, and both came from families with divorced parents and siblings. Nevertheless, they were in love and ready to get married.

Lewis and Jewell pledged their love until death before a host of family and friends on May 4, 1996. Within one year they started having problems, one of which was infertility. Lewis stopped going to church, while Jewell remained a faithful, active member. Within four years they found themselves sleeping in separate bedrooms, not liking one another very much, and estranged as a couple. Jewell found herself separated from her husband and on a spiritual journey. She quickly found out that marriage was nothing like the fairy tales she read as a child.

Jewell accepted the Lord Jesus Christ in 1980 at the age of fourteen. She graduated from VCMI Ministerial Training School in July 2003 and is seeking her Masters of Divinity degree from Regent University.

Lewis Powell, who gave his life to Christ at the tender age of ten, is the CEO of Antiok Holdings Inc., a small minority 8(a) firm headquartered in Southern Maryland. Antiok is an emerging full-service management consulting firm.

Lewis and Jewell have two daughters, Lauren and Diamond. Jewell and Lewis are devoted to having a satisfying and fulfilling marriage and to helping other couples do the same.

If you have testimonies or comments on any material in this book, you may email the author at jewell@marriage101.us.